Acquisition.com Volume II

$100M Leads Summary & Workbook

How to Get Strangers To Want To Buy Your Stuff

ALEX HORMOZI

Acquisition.com, LLC
7710 N FM 620
Building 13C, Suite 100
Austin, Texas 78726

Table of Contents

HOW TO USE THIS WORKBOOK & SUMMARY

Many people buy summaries and workbooks because authors do a poor job editing their fluff. With $100M Leads, this is not the case. It's jam-packed. But, some people would prefer to read it without any stories that drive the points home, and fewer examples. So in this summary, I did five things differently from the book:

1) *Removed* the stories (if you like those, read the main book)

2) *Removed* the majority of examples (if you want more read the main book)

3) *Removed* the majority of transitions and introductions

4) *Removed* explanations behind mechanisms of advertising

5) Replaced the "action steps" with exercises.

The result of which is a summary with exercises that cut the word count of the original book by roughly two thirds. The *main book - $100M Leads -* is about a four hour read. This summary and workbook should take you about one-third of that time (60-90 minutes). If you enjoy it, I *strongly* recommend reading the main book.

If you've already read the book, use this as a review and focus on the exercises.

If you haven't read the main book, you will get what you need to exercise the main concepts in your business.

Use. Get rich. Enjoy. - Alex

SECTION I: START HERE

"It's hard to be poor with leads bangin' down your door"
— Hormozi family jingle

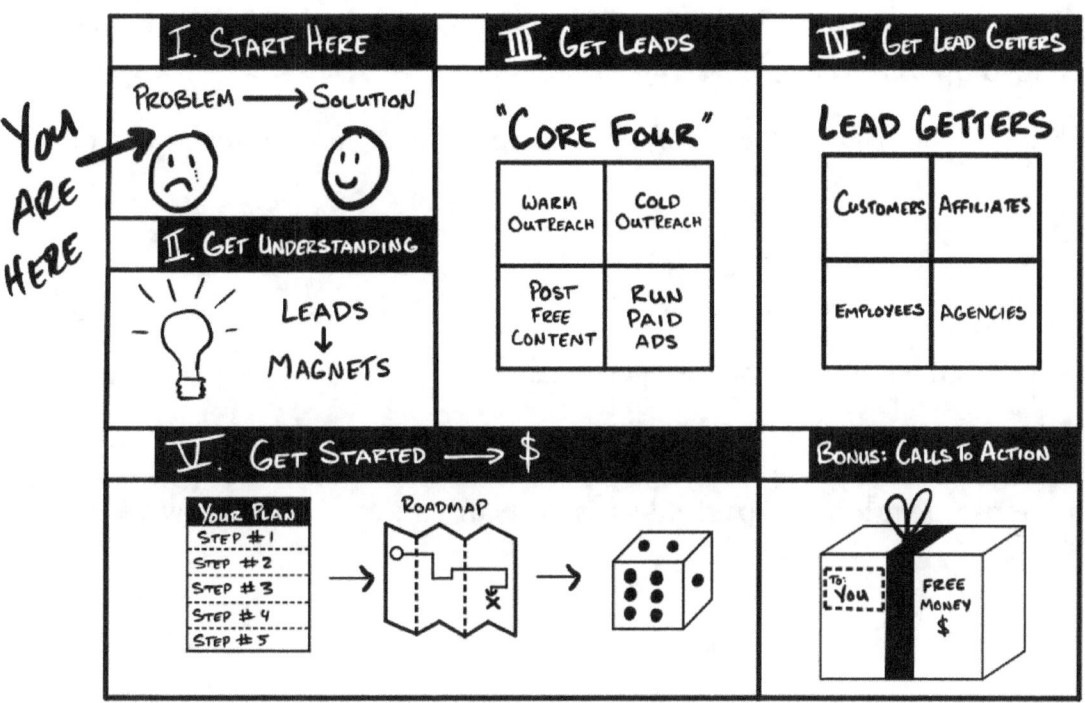

You have to sell stuff to make money. It seems simple enough, but everyone tries to skip to the 'make money' part. It doesn't work. I tried. You need *all* the pieces. You need the stuff to sell - an offer. You need people to sell it to - leads. Then you gotta get those people to buy it - sales. Once you put all those in place, *then* you can make money.

My first book, *$100M Offers,* covers the first step and gives you the *stuff.* It answers the age-old question *"What should I sell?."* Answer - an offer so good people feel stupid saying no. But strangers can only buy your stuff if they know you exist. This takes leads. "Leads" mean a lot of different things to a lot of different people. But most agree that they're the first step to getting more customers. In simpler terms, it means they've got the problem to solve and the money to spend.

If you're reading this book, you already know leads don't magically appear. You need to go get them. More precisely, you need to help them find you so they can buy your stuff! And the best part is, you don't have to wait…you can *force* them to find you. You do that through advertising.

Advertising, *the process of making known*, lets strangers know about the stuff you sell. If more people know about the stuff you sell, then you sell more stuff. If you sell more stuff, then you make more money. *Having lots of leads makes it hard to be poor.*

Advertising lets you have a terrible product... and still make money. It lets you be terrible at sales…and still make money. It lets you make a ton of mistakes and *still. make. money.* In short, having this skill gives you endless chances to *get it right.*

And in the unforgiving world of business, second chances are hard to come by. So you might as well load up. *Advertising is a skill worth having.*

And this book, *$100M Leads Workbook & Summary*, shows you *exactly* how to do it.

Here's How:

First, it explains how advertising works.

Second, it reveals the four core ways to get leads.

Third, it shows you how to get other people to do it for you.

Finally, it wraps up with a one-page advertising plan you can use to grow your business *today*.

Why Listen to Me?

I advertise in a variety of industries through my holding company Acquisition.com. Our portfolio includes software, e-commerce, business services, consumer services, brick & mortar chains, digital products, and plenty of others. Together, they make $250,000,000+ in annual revenue. And they do it by getting 20,000+ leads per day selling offers from $1 to $1,000,000+.

On the personal side, I have a lifetime average return on advertising of 36:1. That means for every $1 I spend on advertising, I get $36 back. A return of 3600%. Some people built their wealth in the stock market. Others in real estate. I built mine *advertising*.

$100M Leads Workbook & Summary is about getting strangers to *show interest* in the stuff you sell. And once I transfer that skill to you, it's your turn to use it.

With that out of the way…let's get rich, shall we?

Pro Tip: Faster, Deeper Learning By Reading & Listening At Same Time

Here's a life hack I stumbled on a years ago. If you listen to an audiobook and read the physical book or ebook at the same time, you read faster *and* remember more. You store the contents in more places in your brain. Nifty stuff. This is **how** I read books worth reading.

I also do both because I struggle to stay focused. If I listen to the audio while reading it helps me avoid zoning out. It took me two days to record this book out loud. I did it so if you struggle like me, you don't have to anymore.

If you want to give it a try, go ahead and grab the audio version and see for yourself. I've made my books as cheap as the platforms let me, so this isn't a ploy to make some extra coin - I promise. I hope you find it as valuable as I have.

I figured I'd put this "hack" early on. This way you'd have a chance to do it if you found the first chapter valuable enough to earn your attention.

Pro Tip: Hack For Finishing Books

I get distracted easily. So I need little tricks to keep my attention. This one helps me alot: <u>Finish chapters. Don't stop in the middle</u>. Completing a chapter gives you positive reinforcement. It keeps you going. So, if you meet a tough chapter, finish it so you can start fresh on the next one.

The Problem This Book Solves

"Leads, lots of leads."

You have a problem: *not enough people know about your stuff. So, you need to advertise more and better.*

How this book solves it:

$100M Leads Workbook & Summary focuses on getting more customers. You get more customers by getting:

1) More Leads

2) Better Leads

3) Cheaper Leads

4) Reliably (think 'from lots of places').

Bottom line: All else being equal…when you double your leads, you double your business.

In a nutshell: I will show you how to get strangers to *want* to buy your stuff.

Basic Outline of This Book

I laid this book out from zero clients, zero leads, zero advertising, zero money, zero skills (Section II) to max clients, max leads, max advertising, max money, and max skills (Section IV). So, we go from getting your first lead all the way to building a $100,000,000+ leads machine. Here's the breakdown:

Section I: *You're about to finish reading it right now.*

Section II: I reveal what makes advertising *really* work.

Section III: We learn advertising's "core four." There are only four ways to get leads. So if there is a most important "how to" section, it's this one.

Section IV: We learn how to get other people (customers, employees, agencies, and affiliates) to do it all for you. And this completes the assembly of your fully functioning *$100M Leads* machine.

Section V: We wrap up with a <u>one-page advertising plan you can use to get more leads today</u>.

GOLDEN TICKET

We invest in companies over $1,000,000+ in profit to help them scale. If you would like us to invest in your business to scale, go to <u>Acquisition.com</u>. You can also find <u>free</u> books and courses so good they grow your business without your consent. And if you don't like typing, you can scan the QR Code below to grab them.

SCAN ME

SECTION II:
GET UNDERSTANDING

Advertising. Simplified.

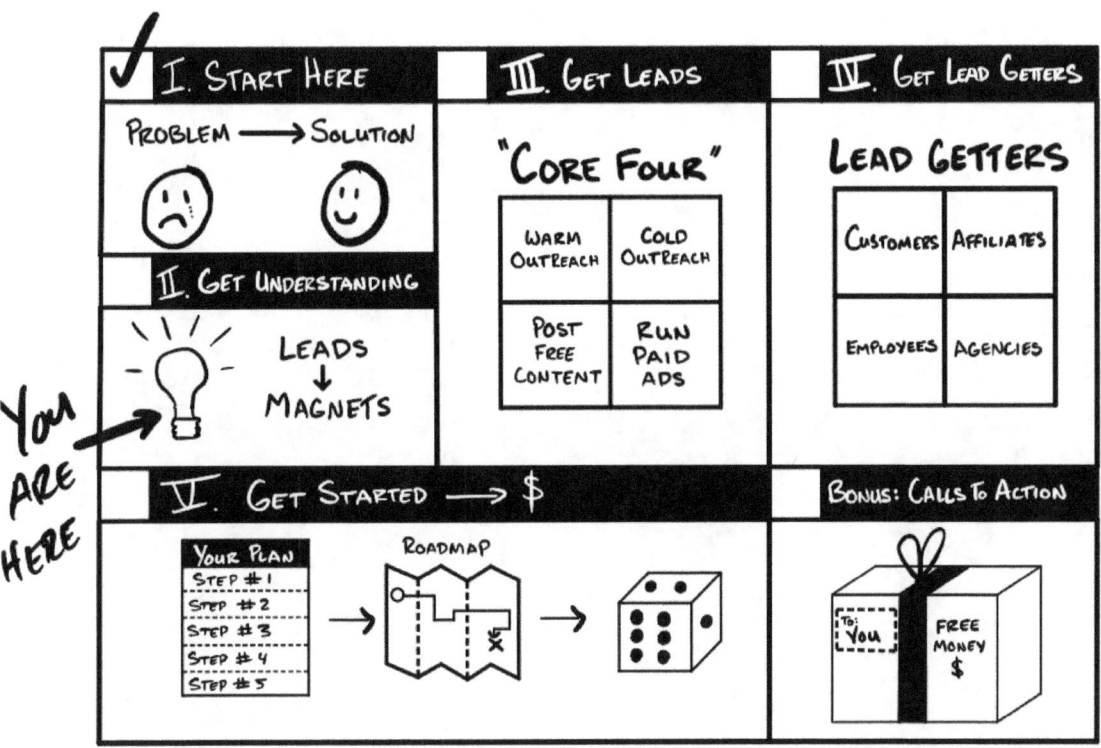

In this section, we cover three things to make sure advertising does exactly what we want it to do.

First, we talk about what a lead actually is. If we want more of them, then we better be darn well sure we're talking about the same thing.

Second, we learn how to separate leads that make you money from leads that waste your time.

Third, I show you the best ways I know to get the leads that make you money to *show interest in the stuff you sell.*

Let's dive in.

Leads Alone Aren't Enough

"If you cannot explain something in simple terms, then you don't understand it."
— *Dr. Richard Feynman, Nobel Prize Winner in Physics*

So what's a lead anyways?

A **lead** is a ***person you can contact***.

Ex: If you bought a list of emails, those are leads. If you get contact information from a website or database, those are leads. The numbers in your phone are leads. People on the street are leads. *If you can contact them, they are leads.*

Leads alone aren't enough...

But what I came to realize was - *leads alone aren't enough*. We want **engaged** leads: *people who *show* interest in the stuff you sell*. If someone *gives* their contact information on a website, that is an engaged lead. If someone *follows* you on social media and you can contact them, that is an engaged lead. If people *reply* to your email campaign, they are engaged leads. The leads *showing interest* are the leads that matter.

Engaged leads are the true output of advertising.

Getting more *engaged* leads is the point of this book. So the next question is: *How do we get leads to engage?*

Engage Your Leads: Offers and Lead Magnets

Lead Magnets Get Leads to Engage

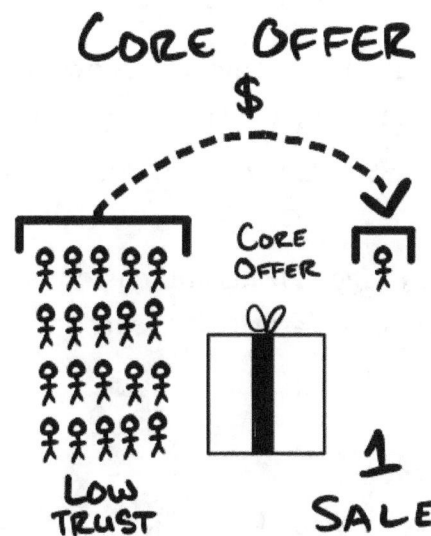

Offers are what you promise to give in exchange for something of value. Often, a business promises to give its product or service in exchange for money. This is a *core offer*. If you advertise your core offer, then you go straight for the sale–the direct path to money. Advertising your core offer might be all you need to get leads to engage. Try this way first.

What to do if advertising your core offer doesn't work immediately...

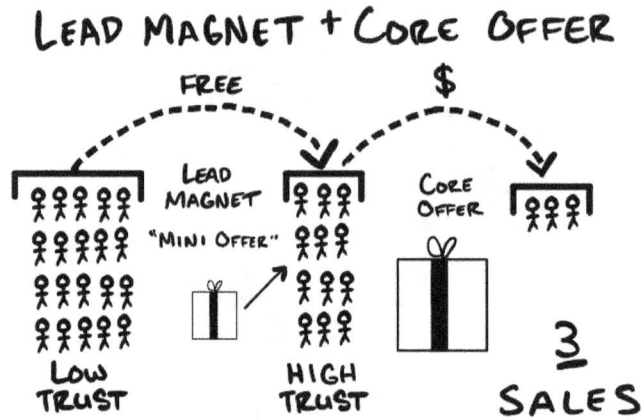

If you sell expensive stuff or people need more information to buy, then you'll get more leads to engage by advertising with a lead magnet first. A **lead magnet** is a <u>complete solution to a narrow problem</u>. It's typically a lower-cost or free offer to see who is interested in your stuff. And, once solved, it reveals another problem *solved by your core offer*. This is important because leads interested in lower-cost or free offers *now* are more likely to buy a related higher-cost offer *later*.

Your lead magnet should be valuable enough on its own that you *could* charge for it. And, after they get it, they should want *more* of what you offer. This gets them one <u>step</u> closer to buying your stuff. *<u>A person who pays with their time now is more likely to pay with their money later.</u>*

Good lead magnets get more engaged leads and customers than a core offer alone, and do it for less money. So let's make a lead magnet, shall we?

Pro Tip: Even Free Stuff Has A Cost

People will give you time before they'll give you money. But, time is still a cost. If your lead magnet isn't worth their time, *it's overpriced*. And, free or not, they won't buy from you again.

So look at it this way—*if they think your lead magnet is* **worth** *their time, they'll think your core offer is worth their money.*

Seven Steps To Creating an Effective Lead Magnet

Step 1: Figure out the problem you want to solve and who to solve it for.

Step 2: Figure out how to solve it

Step 3: Figure out how to deliver it

Step 4: Test what to name it

Step 5: Make it easy to consume

Step 6: Make it darn good

Step 7: Make it easy for them to tell you they want more

Step 1: Figure out the problem you want to solve and who to solve it for

The first step is picking the problem to solve. I use a simple model to figure this out. I call it the Problem-Solution cycle. You can see it below.

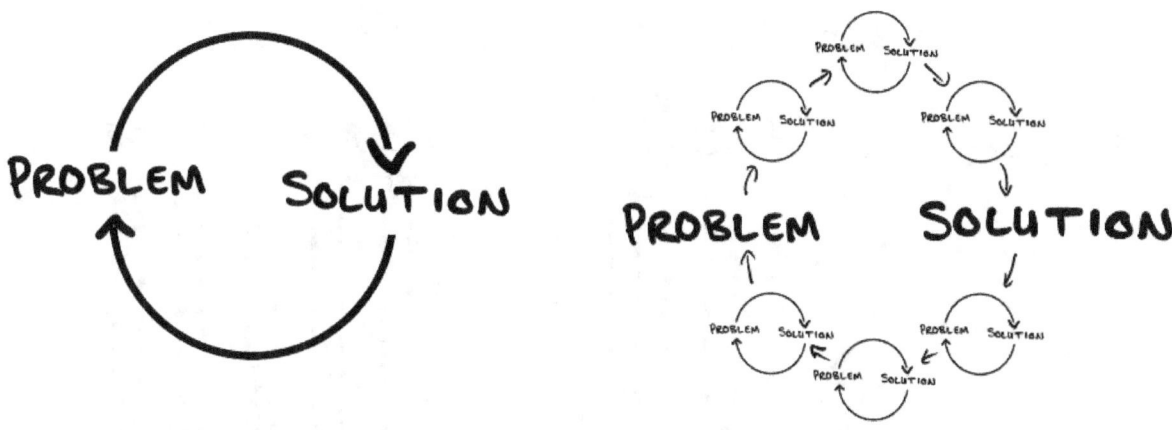

Every problem has a solution. Every solution reveals more problems. We start by picking a problem that's narrow *and* meaningful. Then, solve it. And, like we just learned, when we solve one problem, a new problem reveals itself. Here comes the important part- *if we can solve that new problem with our core offer, we've got a winner.* This is because we solve this new problem *in exchange for money.* That's it. Don't overthink it.

Exercise #1: Pick the narrowly defined problem you want to solve. Then, make sure your core offer can solve the next problem that comes up. Fill in the blanks below.

Narrow problem I will solve: I will help _____ solve their _____ problem. Revealing their _____ problem, solved by my core offer.

Step 2: Figure out how to solve it

There are three types of lead magnets and each offers a different type of solution.

First, if your audience has a problem they don't know about, your lead magnet would make them aware of it. Second, you could solve a recurring problem for a short amount of time with a sample or trial of your core offer. Third, you can give them one step in a multi-step process that solves a bigger problem. All three solve one problem and reveal others. So your three types are: 1) Reveal Problems, 2) Samples and Trials, and 3) One Step Of A Multi-Step Process.

LEAD MAGNET TYPES

#1 REVEAL PROBLEM

#2 FREE TRIAL

#3 FREE STEP 1 OF X

STEP 1 STEP 2 STEP 3 STEP 4 STEP 5

FREE $ $ $ $

1) **Reveal Their Problem.** Think "diagnosis." These lead magnets work great when they reveal problems <u>that get worse the longer you wait.</u> <u>Ex:</u> you run a free speed test on a website and show that they are losing money everyday they don't fix the problem.

2) **Samples And Trials.** You give full but brief access to your core offer. You can limit the number of uses, time they have access, or both. This works great when your core offer

is a recurring solution to a recurring problem. <u>Ex</u>: 14 days of speed enhancement so they see how many more customers they get.

3) **One Step Of A Multi-Step Process**. When your core offer has steps, you can give one valuable step for free and the rest when they buy. This works great when your core offer solves a more complex problem. <u>Ex</u>: This book helps you scale. Then once you scale you have new problems that becoming a portfolio company helps solve.

Exercise #2:   Pick how you want to solve your narrowly defined problem. With…'

☐ An assessment
☐ a sample or trial
☐ single step in a multi-step process.

Step 3: Figure out how to deliver it

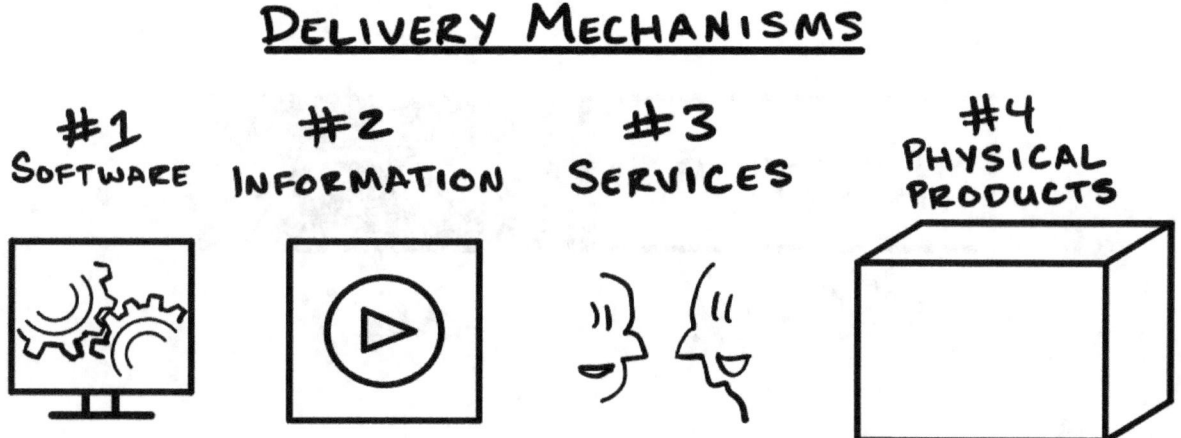

My favorite lead magnets solve problems with: software, information, services, and physical products.

1) <u>Software</u>: *You give them a tool.* If you have a spreadsheet, calculator, or small software, your technology does a job for them.

2) <u>Information</u>: *You teach them something.* Courses, lessons, interviews with experts, keynote presentations, live events, mistakes and pitfalls, hacks/tips, etc. Anything they can <u>learn</u> from.

3) <u>Services</u>: *You do work for free*. Adjust their back. Perform a website audit. Apply the first layer of garage sealant. Transform their video into an ebook. Etc.

4) <u>Physical Products</u>: *You give them something they can hold in their hands*. A posture assessment chart, a supplement, a small bottle of garage door sealant, boxing gloves to get boxing gym leads, etc.

Exercise #3: Write a version of your lead magnet for each delivery method & pick.

☐ Software version: _____

☐ Information version: _____

☐ Service version: _____

☐ Physical product version: _____

Step 4: Test What To Name It

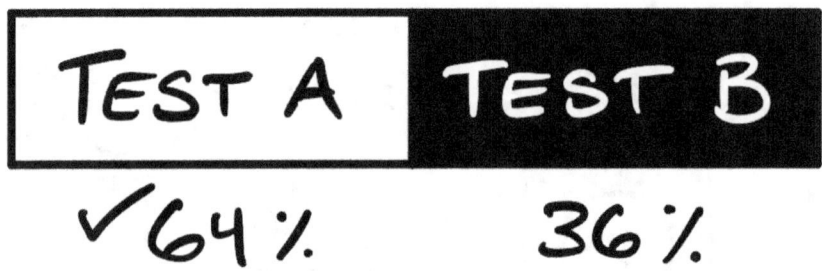

Five times more people read your headline than any other part of your promotion. Leads have to notice your lead magnet *before* they can consume it. This means how we present it matters more than anything. Here's what you do next - <u>you test</u>.

The three things you'll want to test are the headline, the image(s), and the subheadline, in that order. The headline is the most important. So if you only test one thing, test that. For example, I had no idea what to title this book. So here's what I did to figure out which name would do the best - **I tested**. The results may surprise you as much as they surprised me.

Headline Tests

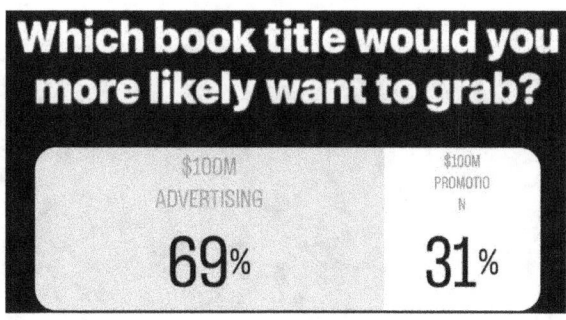

Round I: Advertising ✔ vs Promotion

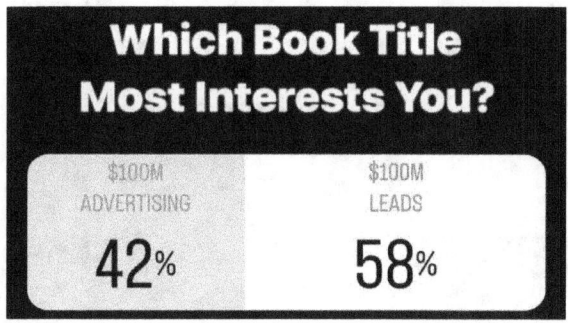

Round II: Advertising vs Leads ✔

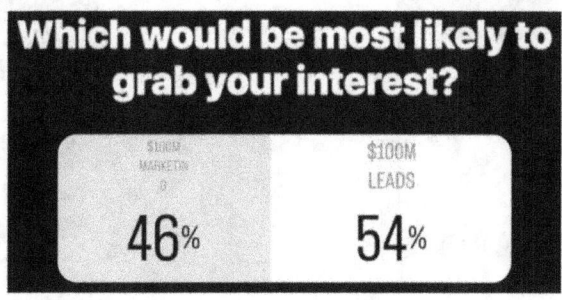

Round III: Marketing vs Leads ✔

Image Test

✔ Real vs. Cartoon

Subheadlines

Round I:

"How to get more people to want to buy your stuff"

"How to get strangers to want to buy your stuff" ✔

Round II:

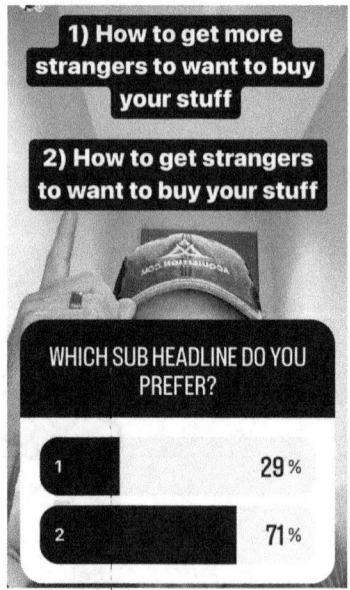

How to get more strangers to want to buy your stuff"

"How to get strangers to want to buy your stuff" ✔

Round III:

Round IV:

"How to get as many leads as you darn well please"

"How to get strangers to want to buy your stuff" ✔

"Get strangers to want to buy your stuff"

"How to get strangers to want to buy your stuff" ✔

Exercise #4: Come up with 3-4 names for your lead magnet. Then test it.

☐ If you have any following at all, run a poll like the examples.

☐ If you can't do that, make a post on every platform and ask people to respond with a '1' or a '2', then tally the votes for each.

☐ If you still can't even do that, then just message people and ask: A or B?

Step 5: Make it easy for them to consume

People prefer to do things that take less effort. So, we gotta make it easy to consume our lead magnet. **Here's how you can make each delivery mechanism easier:**

1) Software: You want to make it accessible on their phones, on a computer and in multiple different formats. This way, they'll pick the one easiest for them.

2) Information: People like to consume things in different ways. Some people like watching, other people like reading, others like listening, etc. Make your solution in as many different formats as you can: images, video, text, audio, etc. Offer them all.

3) Services: Be available at more times in more ways. More times of day. More days of the week. Via video call, phone call, in person, etc. The easier you are to get a hold of, the more likely people will become engaged leads to claim the free value.

4) Physical products: Make it super simple to order and fast to get to them. Make the product itself fast and easy to open. Give simple directions on how to use the product.

Exercise #5: Based on the delivery method from Exercise #3, and the information above, make your lead magnet as easy as possible to consume so more leads do.

Step 6: Make it darn good:

Give Away The Secrets, Sell The Implementation

The marketplace judges everything you have to offer - *free or not*. And you can never provide too much value. But, you *can* provide too little. So you want your lead magnet to provide so much value people feel obligated to pay you. The goal is to provide more value than the cost of your core offer *before they've bought it.*

Don't be afraid of giving away too much value. Be afraid of giving away too little and people finding out.

> **Exercise #6: Write out the cost of your core offer: $_____.**
>
> Make sure your lead magnet provides more value to them than that amount.

Step 7: Make it easy for them to tell you they want more

Once the leads consume the lead magnet, some of them will be ready to buy or learn more about your offer. This is the time to give a Call To Action. A **Call To Action (CTA)** *tells the audience what to do next.* Good CTAs have two things: 1) what to do and 2) reasons to do it *right now.*

What to do: CTAs tell the audience to call the number, click the button, give information, book the call, etc. There are way too many to list. Just know CTAs tell the audience how to become engaged leads. Good CTAs have clear, simple, and direct language. Not *"don't delay"* but instead *"call now."*

Reasons to do it right now - If you give people a reason to take action, more people will do it. But a couple of things to keep in mind: first, good reasons work better than bad reasons. And second, any reason (even bad ones) tends to work better than no reason at all. So to get more people to take action, I include as many effective reasons as I can. Here are my favorite reasons to act now:

a) **Scarcity**- Scarcity *is when there is a limited amount of something.*

b) **Urgency**. **Urgency** *is when people act faster because they have a short amount of time.* You can have unlimited units to sell, but let's say you stop selling them in an hour… *on purpose.* The less time people have, the faster (more urgent) they tend to act. So if you make the time they can act on your CTA shorter, you can get *more* of them to act on it *faster*. You can also use the same urgency with discounts or bonuses that go away after X minutes or hours. After which, this offer will never be available again.

c) **Fraternity Party Planner (my favorite) - Make Up A Reason**. Fraternities don't need a reason to party - but they sure make up some doozies. "John got his wisdom teeth removed…kegger!" "Margherita Monday!" "Toga Tuesdays" "Thirsty Thursday!" etc. Your reason doesn't even have to make sense, *and it will still* get more people to act.

Exercise #7: Add in features to your lead magnet to make a compelling CTA.

Simple clear CTA: _____

Reason to do it now (urgency and/or scarcity): _____
_____

Why use a lead magnet to begin with

Even if your lead magnet costs money to deliver, it should still *lower* your cost to get a new customer. This is because more engaged leads means more chances to get customers. And the extra customers *more than* cover your costs. That's the point.

If you used to get 5 people to buy directly, you might create 100 leads for the same cost and get ten percent of them to buy. This means you double your sales by *adding* a lead magnet to your advertising.

Action Steps:

Step 0: If you're struggling to get leads, make an <u>amazing</u> lead magnet.

Step 1: Figure out the problem you want to solve for the right customer

Step 2: Figure out how you want to solve it

Step 3: Figure out how to deliver it

Step 4: Make the name interesting and clear

Step 5: Make it easy to consume

Step 6: Make sure it's darn good

Step 7: Tell them what to do next, why it's a good idea, do it clearly, and do it often

> **Exercise #8: Combine answers from Exercises 1-7.** Now you have your lead magnet.

Section II Conclusion

My goal with this workbook is to demystify the lead-getting process. In the first chapter, we covered why leads alone aren't enough–you need *engaged leads*. In the second chapter, we covered how to get leads to engage - *a valuable lead magnet or offer*. And a good lead magnet does four things:

1) Engages ideal customers when they see it.

2) Gets more people to engage than your core offer alone

3) Is valuable enough that they consume it.

4) Makes the right people more likely to buy

So, more people show interest in our stuff. We make more money from them. And we deliver more value than we ever have–all at the same time.

Next Up:

We've armed ourselves with a powerful lead magnet. Now, I'll show you the four ways we can advertise it. In other words, now that we have "the stuff,"–we gotta tell people about it. Let's get some leads.

FREE GIFT: Bonus Tutorial on Making The Ultimate Lead Magnet

If you want a more in depth look at how we create insanely good lead magnets, go to acquisition.com/training/leads. It's free and publicly available. As promised, my goal is to earn your trust. And trust is built brick by brick. Allow this training to be the first of many bricks. Enjoy. You can also scan the QR code below if you hate typing.

SECTION III: GET LEADS

The Core Four Advertising Methods.

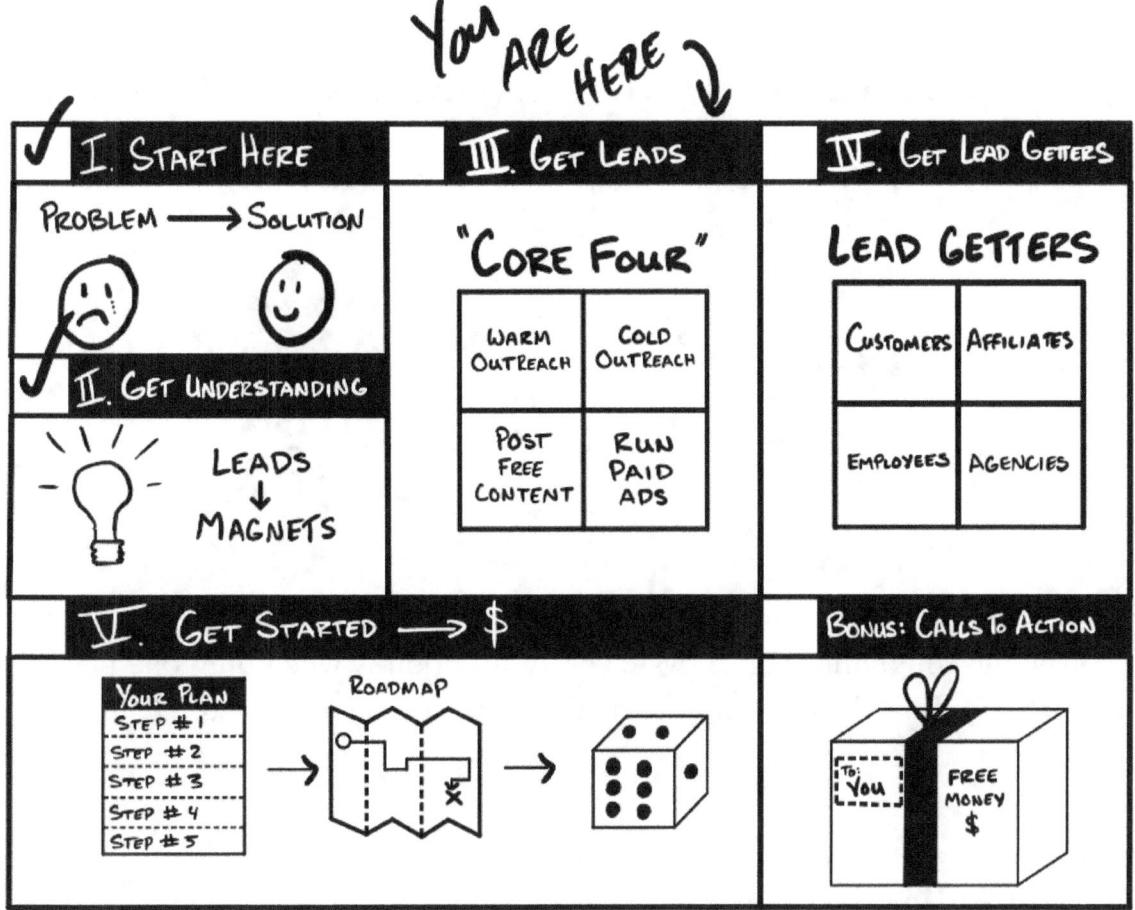

We get engaged leads by letting people know about our stuff. And there are two types of people we let know: people who know us and people who don't. And there are two paths of letting them know about it: one-to-one and one-to-many. Those combine into the four basic ways one person can let other people know about anything. Let's break down how we can use those four ways to get us leads.

Two Types of Audiences: Warm and Cold

Warm audiences are *people who gave you permission to contact them.* Think "people who know you" - aka - friends, family, followers, current customers, previous customers, contacts, etc.

Cold audiences are *people who have not given you permission to contact them.* Think "strangers" - aka - other peoples' audiences: buying contact lists, making contact lists, paying platforms for access, etc.

The difference matters because it changes *how* we advertise to them.

Two Ways To Communicate: One to One (Private), One to Many (Public)

We can contact people 1-to-1 or 1-to-many. Another way of thinking about this is private or public communication. Private communication is when only one person gets a message at a time. Think "phone call" or "email." If you announce something publicly, many people can get it at the same time. Think "social media posts" or "billboards" or "podcasts."

Section III Outline: Get Leads

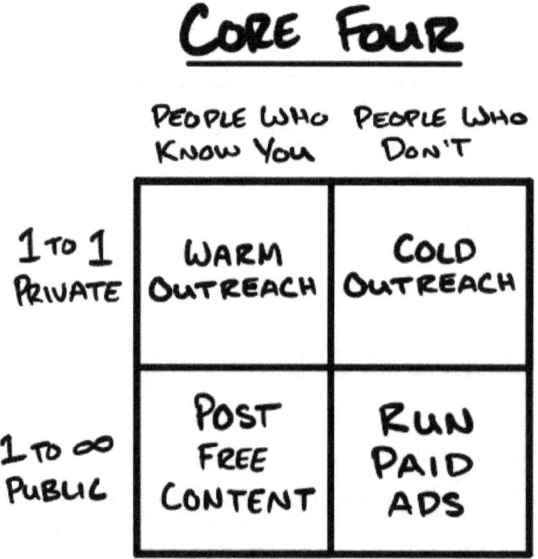

Combining warm and cold audiences with 1-to-1 and 1-to-many leads us to the only four ways we can let anyone know about anything: the core four. I combined them below for you.

- 1-to-1 to a Warm Audience = Warm Outreach

- 1-to-many to a Warm Audience = Posting Content

- 1-to-1 to a Cold Audience = Cold Outreach

- 1-to-many to a Cold Audience = Paid Ads

These are the *only* four things you can <u>do</u> to let other people know about the stuff you sell. So if you aren't getting as many leads as you want, you're not doing the core four with enough skill or with enough volume.

FREE GIFT: Bonus Training - The Core Four Framework

I did a live training where I explained the 50+ iterations that created this simple 2 x 2 box. I explain how to use the core four framework to get the most leads possible and create goals within your company. If you want it, you can get it fo' free here: Acquisition.com/training/leads. You can also scan the QR code below if you hate typing.

#1 Warm Outreach

How To Reach Out To People You Know

"The world belongs to those who can keep doing without seeing the result of their doing."

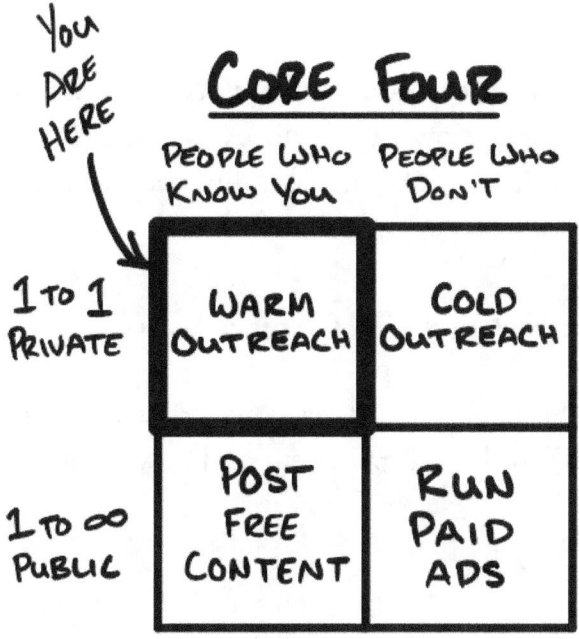

How Warm Reach Outs Work

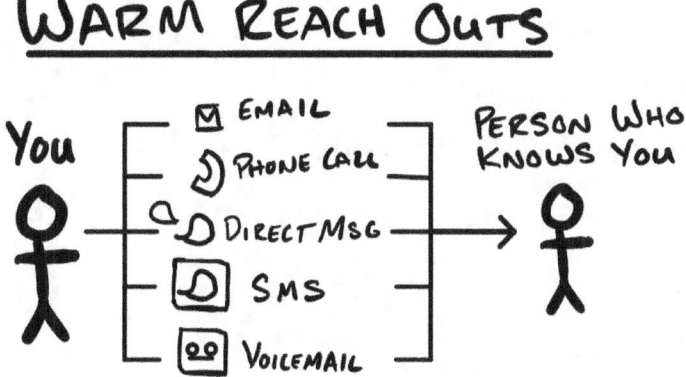

Warm reach outs are when you make one-to-one contact with your warm audience - aka - the people who know you. It's the cheapest and easiest way to find people interested in the stuff you sell. Also, everyone has a warm audience, even if you don't know it. Everybody knows somebody. So your personal contacts are the easiest place to start.

Warm reach outs usually come in the form of calls, texts, emails, direct messages, voice-mails, etc. You let them know about your lead magnet (something free and valuable), or you let them know about your core offer (the main thing you sell).

When you start doing warm reach outs, you don't get many engaged leads for your time. You do everything on your own and make each message personal. But, for that reason, it is *reliable*.

<u>Note:</u> Reaching out to your warm audience works whether you have 100 contacts or 1,000,000. So as your business grows, you will use automation and employees to make it more efficient. The systems start small, with you, but they scale *all the way up*.

How To Do Warm Reach Outs in 10 Steps

Warm reach outs are a fantastic way to get your "First Five Clients" *For any new product or service.* Advanced Folks: Think re-engagement and new product lines. Here's how to do it:

Step 1: Get your list

Step 2: Pick a platform

Step 3: Personalize your message

Step 4: Reach out

Step 5: Warm them up

Step 6: Invite their friends

Step 7: Make them the easiest offer in the world

Step 8: Start at the top

Step 9: Start Charging

Step 10: Keep Your List Warm

(Step 1) "But I don't have any leads…" → Everyone Has A List

You know other humans. Let me prove it to you.

- Grab your phone. Inside you have contacts. *Each contact has subscribed to communication from you.* They have given you the means *and permission* to contact them.

- Pull up *all* the email accounts you've used over the years. Pull your contacts and address list from each. Bingo! Look at all them leads.

- Now, go to all your social media profiles. See your followers, subscribers, friends, connections, or whatever kids call 'em these days…eureka - you got more leads!

Exercise #9: Add up <u>all</u> your contacts from <u>all</u> the platforms including your phone, email, social media, and other platforms. For most, this will be your first 1000 leads.

And if you're terrified you'll have to talk to people. Relax. You'll like what I'm gonna show you next.

(Step 2) "But I don't know where to start…" → Pick A Platform

Exercise #10: Pick the platform you have the most contacts on from Exercise #9.

(Step 3) "But what do I say?" → Personalize your greeting

Exercise #11: Write down something personal you know about each lead. Either from the top of your head, or based on a quick online search. You can start with just the first 100 leads.

Note: Remember, you haven't asked for anything. You're just checking in and providing value. *So…relax.* Ex: *Saw you just had a baby! Congrats! How is the baby doing? How are you?*

(Step 4) "Now what?" → Reach. Out. To. One. Hundred. People. Every. Day.

"To get what you want, you have to deserve what you want." - Charlie Munger

Exercise #12: Reach out to 100 leads per day with your personalized message from Exercise #11. Reach out up to 1x per day for 3 days, or until they reply.

(Step 5): "What do I say when they respond?" → Act like a human.

Now we can break the ice without sounding icky.

Reply using the **A-C-A** framework:

- Acknowledge what they said. Restate it in your own words. This shows active listening.

  o *Ex: Two kids. And you're an accountant…*

- Compliment them on whatever they tell you. Tie it to a positive character trait if you can.

  o *Ex: …Wow! Supermom! So hardworking! Managing a full-time career and two kids…*

- Ask another question. Lead the conversation in whatever direction you want. In this case, to a topic closer to your offer. Examples:

o Therapy/Life Coaching: …*Do you get time for yourself?*

o Fitness/Weight Loss:…*Do you have time to get workouts in?*

o Cleaning Services:…*Do you have anyone who helps you keep the house tidy?*

The ACA framework is great because it helps you talk to anyone. It just so happens it's *also* useful for letting people know about your stuff. This means you can learn about the person *and* guide the conversation toward your offer.

Pro Tip: On Email You'll Be More Up Front

On email you will have a personalized opener to show that you actually took time to research them in some way. Think 2-3 sentences. Then, you will transition directly to your offer or lead magnet which we talk about next. You sort of 'do it all at once' with email or voicemails.

(Step 6) "How do I know if they're interested?" → Make them an offer.

Get through a 'normal' amount of conversation. Think 3-4 exchanges if on the phone or messaging and 3-4 minutes if in person. Then, you'll make them an offer to see if they're interested.

When I make an offer from scratch, I refer to the value equation. If you're wondering 'what's the value equation?' - it was the core concept of my first book *$100M Offers*. Value, as I define it, has four elements:

1) <u>Dream Outcome</u>: what the person wants to happen, the way they want it to happen

- State the best possible results your product can get. Big bonus points if those results come from people like the one you're talking to.

2) <u>Perceived Likelihood of Achievement</u>: how likely they think it is for them to achieve their goal

- Include results, reviews, awards, endorsements, certifications, and other forms of *3rd party validation*. Also, guarantees are huge.

3) <u>Time Delay</u>: how long they believe it'll take to get results after they buy

- Describe how fast people *start* getting results, how often they get results when they start, and how long it takes to get the best results possible.

4) <u>Effort and Sacrifice</u>: The bad stuff they'll have to endure and the good stuff they'll have to give up in their struggle to get the result.

- Show them the good stuff they can keep doing, or get to do, and still get results. And show them the bad stuff that they can get rid of, or avoid doing, and still get results.

The goal is to maximize the first two and minimize the second two. So all you have to do now is show someone:

- You have exactly what they want

- They're guaranteed to get it

- Insanely fast

- Without lifting a finger or giving up anything they love

So let's do just that with a real-life offer:

...By the way, <u>do you know anybody</u> who is (describe their struggles) *looking to* (dream outcome*) in* (time delay)*? I'm taking on five case studies for free, because that's all I can handle. I just want to get some testimonials for my service/product. I help them* (dream outcome*) without* (effort and sacrifice)*. It works. I even guarantee people get* (dream outcome) *or I work with them until they do. I just had a girl named XXX work with me* (dream outcome) *even though she* (describe the same struggle your contact has)*. I also had another guy who* (dream outcome) *and it was his first time. I'd just like more testimonials to show it works across different scenarios. Does anyone you like come to mind?* (Pause if on the phone) *...and if they say no...Haha, well... does anyone you <u>hate</u> come to mind?* (ha) This helps break any awkwardness.

Note: *We're not asking them to buy anything. We're asking if they know anyone.* Since you didn't ask them to buy anything, you don't come off as pushy. And of the people who say yes, most say *they* are interested. Some people will show interest in your stuff. Some will refer you to those who might. Some will do both. In all three outcomes, you win. And you win *without pushing anything on anyone.*

Value message: *I help* (ideal customer) *get* (dream outcome) *in* (time period) *without* (effort and sacrifice) *and* (increase perceived likelihood of achievement–look at the pro tip below).

Note: These work well for emails, texts, direct messages, calls, and in-person. Just fill in the blanks.

Exercise #13: Create your value message. *I help:*

(ideal customer) _____

get (dream outcome) _____

in (time period) _____

without (effort and sacrifice) _____

and (increase perceived likelihood of achievement) _____

_____

Pro Tip: 11 Ways To Increase Perceived Likelihood of Achievement

Here's how you increase their perceived likelihood of achievement so more people take you up on your offer. Include one or more of the following:

1. Showing proof we have done what they want (our own story)

2. Showing proof of people *just like them* getting what they want (think testimonials)

3. Showing the sheer volume of happy reviews we've received (think lots of 5-stars)

    a. If you don't have reviews yet, even the number of people you've helped works.

4. Certifications/Degrees/Third party accreditations that we're legit

5. Numbers, stats, research that supports the outcome you want them to believe

6. Experts vouching for us

7. Some new/unique characteristic they haven't failed with before (so it might work this time)

8. Celebrities who have endorsed us ('they trusted them, so should I')

9. Guaranteeing they'll achieve it (so we put some skin in the game too)

10. How well you describe them or the current pain they're experiencing. The more specific the better. (think 'he/she really gets me, they must know how to help')

11. If possible, demonstrate the outcome live. Or, show a recording of it happening.

    a. Ex: Advertising agency plays a recording of a call that a gym owner has to make to a lead on the sales call. "Could you handle making a call like that to a lead if we get them for you?" It demonstrates the outcome of the advertising services - people don't want "leads" they want customers. They just don't know a better way to ask for them.

(Step 7) "How do I get them to say yes?" → Make it easy for them to say yes. Make it free.

My recommendation - whenever you launch a new product or service - make the first five free. The exact number matters less than knowing why you benefit from it. Here's why:

1) You get the reps in and become comfortable with making offers to people. It'll calm your nerves knowing you're just helping…for free…for now (winky face).

2) You probably suck (for now). People are far more forgiving when you haven't charged anything.

3) Because you probably suck, you need to learn how to suck less. You suck less by doing more. It's better to have a few guinea pigs to get the kinks out. You'll learn a ton from the people you help for free, I promise. Even though it may not feel like it now, you're getting the better end of the deal.

4) If people get value, especially for free, they're far more likely to:

    a) Leave positive reviews and testimonials.

    b) Give you feedback.

    c) Send their friends and family.

And if that's not awesome enough, free customers can make you money in three other ways:

    1) They convert into paying customers.

    2) They send you paying customers via referrals.

    3) Their testimonials bring in paying customers.

So no matter what, you win.

Here's what I say:

Since I'm only taking on five people, I can give you all the attention you need to get brag-worthy results. And I'll give it all for free so long as you promise to: 1) Use it 2) Give me feedback and 3) Leave a killer review if you think it deserves one. Does that sound fair?

Pro Tip: Apply the "Hinge Method" to Referrals

If you ask for a referral, get a three-way introduction. My favorite way to do this in person is to grab the customer's phone, take a picture of the two of us, then text that picture to the referral <u>and</u> your own number. If I'm virtual, screenshot a video call and do the same thing. If you can't do that, then at least get a three way conversation going with *them* initiating it.

What if they say no?

Often, the most expensive part of what you sell isn't the price–it's the hidden costs. **Hidden costs** are the time, effort, and sacrifice it takes to get results from the thing you sell. In other words, <u>the bottom part of the value equation</u>. If you struggle to give your stuff away for free, it means either people don't want it (dream outcome), they don't believe you (perceived likelihood of achievement) *or* the hidden costs (time, effort and sacrifice) are too high. In short, your 'free' stuff is *too expensive*. So figure out the hidden costs. Once you do, you unlock even more value–that you'll eventually be able to charge for.

(Step 8) "What Do I Do Once I've Reached Out To Everyone?" → Start Back At The Top

After reaching out to all the leads on one platform, switch to the platform you have the second most leads on. After you reach out to those leads, go to the platform you have the third most leads on and so forth.

(Step 9) "But I can't work for free forever…" → Start Charging.

After reaching out to all the leads on one platform, switch to the platform you have the second most leads on. After you reach out to those leads, go to the platform you have the third most leads on and so forth.

This is important. This is your litmus test to know when you're "good enough" to charge. *Once people start referring, start charging.* When that happens, swap out '… *free…*' in the script above to '*80% off* for the next five'. Then 60% off for the next five. Then 40% off for the next five, and so forth. Feel free to keep raising it by 20% every five until you find your sweet spot.

Pro Tip: Get More Cash Up Front & More Yeses → Prepay + Guarantee

Offering a guarantee gets more people to buy because it reverses risk. Here's a nice twist on a guarantee that'll get you more yeses *and* more cash.

You can offer a guarantee only to people who pay up front. Reason why: *People who invest up front are more committed. And as a result, we're able to guarantee their outcomes. So if you'd like our guarantee, you can prepay our service.*

Another version of wording I got my good friend Dr. Kashey: After the person agrees to buy, you say *"would you rather pay less today or get all your money back?"* Paying less today = payment plan, so less money down. Get all your money back = prepay and get a guarantee that you get the result you want.

> Ex: "Pay Less" = $2000/mo for 3 months = $6000 (no guarantee)
>
> Or
>
> "Get All Your Money Back" = $6000 up front *with* a guarantee.

Presented this way, the majority of the people take the up front cash option with the guarantee. So if you planned on offering one anyways, you may as well weaponize it to incentivize more people to pay up front.

(Step 10) "But what do I do from here?" →Keep your list warm.

Give regular value to your list through email, social media, etc. to keep it warm. A warm list stays primed for your warm reach outs in the future. Once you've given value for a while, or see who wants value, probe your list with Dean Jackson's timeless "9-word email" template:

Are you still looking to [4 word desire]?

And *these replies should be your top priority for warm reach outs.*

If you keep providing value, your audience will feed you forever.

Exercise #14: Write your one-line message.

Are you still looking to _____

_____ ?

Advertising Checklist Summary

Now let's look at this in ten lines because it took a few pages to get here.

Warm Reach Outs Daily Checklist	
Who:	Yourself
What:	First five free
Where:	Phone/Email/Physical Mail/SMS/Etc
To Whom:	Your Contacts
When:	First four hours of your day
Why:	You want to get customers or intros
How:	Personalized Message using ACA
How Much:	100 Attempts Per Day
How Many:	Follow up two more times after first.
How Long:	Until you get customers

Benchmarks: How well am I doing?

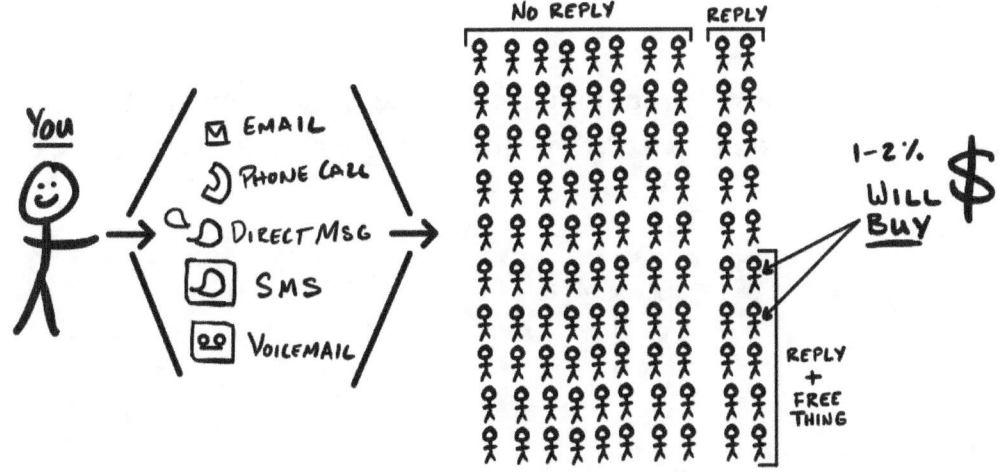

Warm reach outs should get about one in five contacts to engage. So one hundred warm reach outs should get about twenty replies. Of the twenty who reply, another one in five*ish* will take you up on your free offer. So, four people. Of the four who take your free offer now, you should be able to convert *one* into some sort of paid offer later.

This process *alone* can take you to $100,000+ per year with nothing else. Here's the money math:

This assumes that 1% of your list buys a $400 offer using *only* warm reach outs.

500 reach outs per week = 5 customers per week

$400 product → 5 customers per week x $400 each = $2000/wk

$2000/wk x 52 weeks = $104,000…bingo.

Which, as of this writing, is still two times the median household income in the US. Not bad.

Pro Tip: Join Communities

To learn even faster, join communities of people doing the same advertising method as you. They're great for peer support and up-to-date tricks and tips. Also - don't do anything sketchy. There are lots of people who pride themselves on pushing the legal envelope. Don't be that person. It always comes back to bite you. Do it the right way and you will feed yourself for life.

What's Next?

Warm reach outs have two limitations. Time and the number of people you know. So, next, we *add* the second of the core four advertising activities: posting free content.

FREE GIFT: Bonus Training - Warm Reach Outs

If you like this stuff, I go deeper in a no-holds-barred breakdown of the many different strategies you can use within warm reach outs to get your first or zillionth customer. If that sounds cool, go to Acquisition.com/ training/leads. And, if you needed another reason, it's free. I hope you use it to get as many leads as you need. You can also scan the QR code below if you hate typing.

#2 Post Free Content Part I

How To Build An Audience To Get Engaged Leads

No one's ever complained about getting too much value.

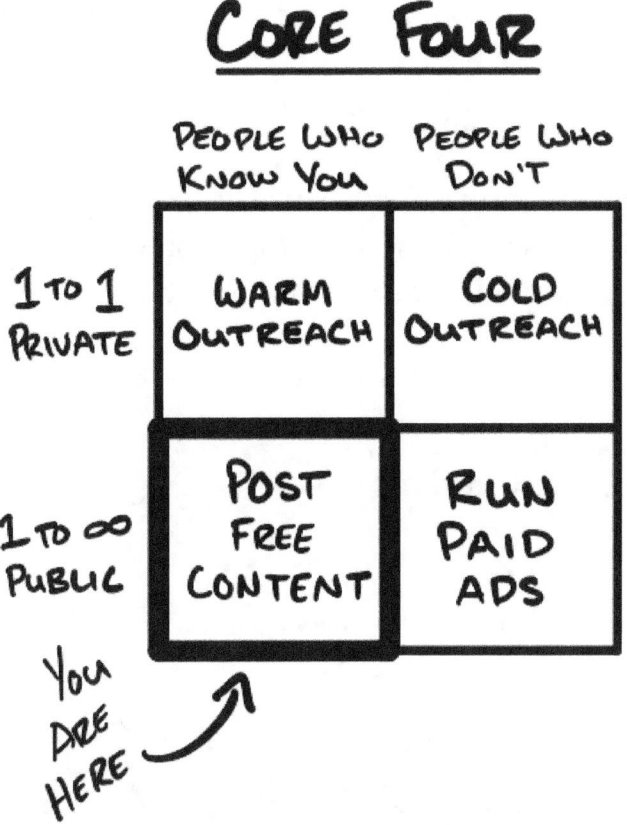

How Building An Audience Works - You Post Great Free Content

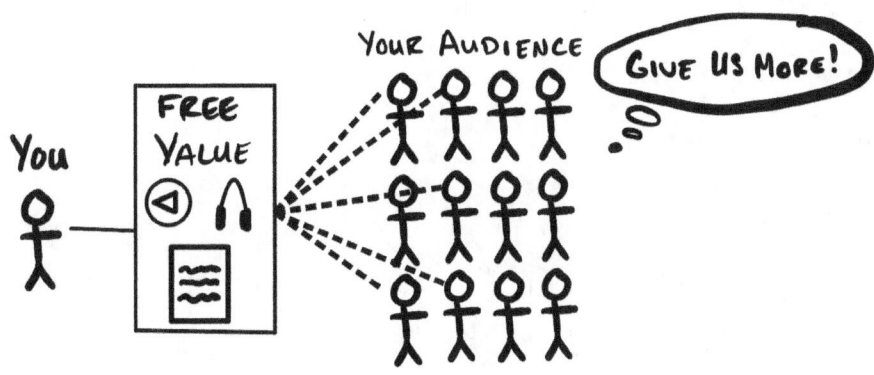

Posting free content can get a lot more engaged leads for the time we invest. The people who think it's valuable become part of your warm audience. If they think other people will find it valuable, they share it. And if the people they share it with like it, they become part of your warm audience too.

What makes posting content hard. First, it is more difficult to personalize your message. So fewer people respond. Second, you compete with everyone else posting free content. This makes it harder to stand out. Third, if you do stand out, people will copy you. This means you need to constantly innovate.

What makes it worth it. A bigger audience means more engaged leads.

What's inside this chapter. First, we demystify audience-growing content by showing it's all made of the same basic units. A content unit has three components - Hook, retain, and reward. Second, how linking basic units together will make audience-growing content for any platform or media type.

The Content Unit - Three Components

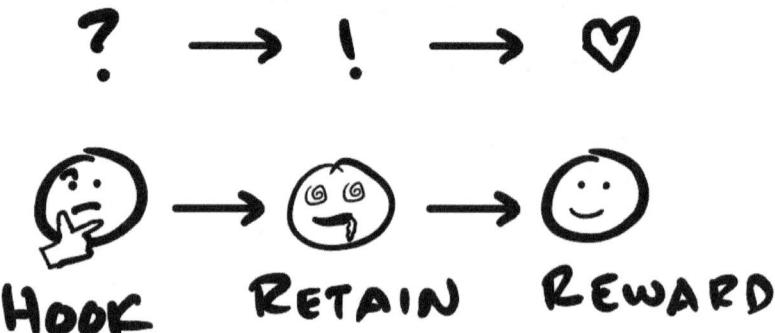

All audience-growing content does one thing - it rewards the people consuming it. And a person can only get rewarded by the content if they:

1) Have a reason to consume it and

2) Pay attention long enough to

3) Get that reason satisfied.

Thankfully, we can reverse those three outcomes into the three things we have to *do* to make audience-growing content. This means we have to:

a) **Hook** attention: get them to notice your content

b) **Retain** attention: get them to consume it.

c) **Reward** attention: satisfy the reason they consumed it to begin with.

The smallest amount of material it takes to hook, retain and reward attention is a **content unit**. It can be as little as an image, a meme, or a sentence. Meaning, you can hook, retain, and reward *at the same time*.

1) Hook: They cannot be rewarded unless we first get their attention.

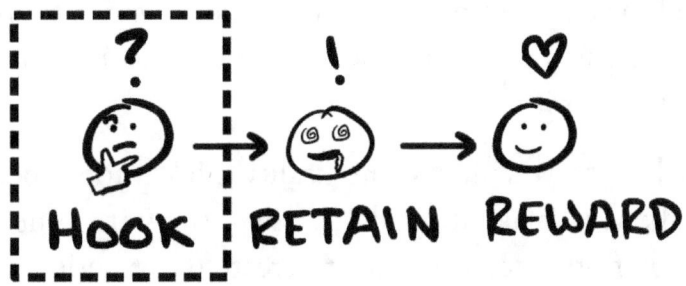

The objective: We give them a reason to redirect their attention from whatever they are doing towards us. If we do that, we've hooked them. The effectiveness of your hook is measured by the percentage of people who start consuming your content. So if you hook attention well, *many* people will have a reason to consume your content. If you do a poor job, *few* people will have a reason to consume your content.

Hook components. We increase the percentage of people who pick our content by picking *topics* they find interesting, *headlines* that give them a reason, and matching the *format* of other stuff they like.

Topics. Topics are the things you make your content about. I prefer to use personal experiences. I divide topics into five categories: Far Past, Recent Past, Present, Trending, and Manufactured.

a) <u>Far Past</u>: The important *past* lessons in your life. Connect that wisdom to your product or service to provide huge value to your audience. Give them the story without the scar.

b) <u>Recent Past</u>: Do stuff, then talk about what you did (or what happened). Look at your calendar for the last week. Look at all your meetings. Look at all your social interactions. Look at all your conversations with warm reach outs. *There's gold in these conversations.* Tell stories from them that would serve your audience.

    i)   This means taking notes, recordings, and other records to make that stuff easy to access. But it also means a free, easy, and valuable stash of content.

    ii)   Testimonials and case studies fall in this category. If you can tell a cool client story *in a way that provides value to your audience*, you'll both promote your services and provide value.

c) <u>Present</u>: Write down ideas *at the exact time they come to you*. Always have a way to record your ideas in arms reach. I'll even pause meetings to make note of, text, or email ideas to myself.

d) <u>Trending</u>: Talking about trendy stuff is very effective for gaining the attention of a broader audience. If you have relevant commentary or it touches your expertise in some way, talk about it.

e) <u>Manufactured</u>: Turn your ideas into reality. Pick a topic people find interesting. Then, learn about it, make it, or do it. Then, show it to the world. This costs the most time and effort since you have to create the experience versus talking about one you already had. But, it can have the biggest payouts.

    i)   Example manufactured experience: *I lived on $100 for a month. Here's how.*

    ii)   **Manufactured vs Documenting.** Manufactured grows audiences the most because skilled content creators can engineer the maximum reward for every content unit. But, it costs more than documenting. So, do the one you can for now.

Exercise #15: Look at your calendar. Write down the interesting stories that happened to you over the past two weeks. The things you learned, failed at, succeeded with.

Cool story: _____

Cool lesson: _____

Failure: _____

Big epiphany: _____

_____

Headlines. A headline is a short phrase or sentence used to grab the audience's attention. It communicates the reason they should consume the content. They use it to weigh the likelihood they will get a reward for consuming your content versus another.

Seven things that make headlines more interesting.

a. Recency - As recent as possible, quite literally the 'new's. Now vs a year ago.

b. Relevancy - Personally meaningful. Applies to them versus doesn't.

c. Celebrity - Including prominent people (celebrities, authorities, etc.). About a celebrity vs about a normal person.

d. Proximity - Close to home - geographically. Next door vs across the world.

e. Conflict - of opposing ideas, opposing people, nature, etc. Ex: politics.

f. Unusual - odd, unique, rare, bizarre. Six-fingered man vs five-fingered man.

g. Ongoing - Stories still in progress are dynamic, evolving, and have plot twists.

Exercise #16: Write a headline for each of the stories from Exercise #15 using 2-3 of the headline elements above.

Cool story: _____

Cool lesson: _____

Failure: _____

Big epiphany: _____

_____

Format. We need to match our format to the best content on the platform.

<u>Format example:</u>

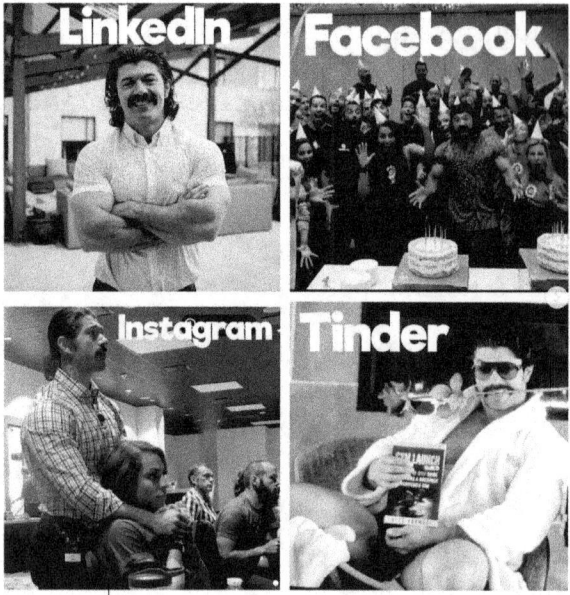

This meme has the same person (me) on four different platforms. Each matched to the platform format.

> **Exercise #17: Look at the highest performing content on four platforms. Format one piece of content for four different platforms, according to the best styles of each.**

2) Retain

My favorite driver of retention is *curiosity*. My three favorite ways to drive curiosity are: lists, steps, and stories.

a) Lists: Lists are things, facts, tips, opinions, ideas, etc. presented one after the other following a theme. Giving the number of listed items in your headline, or in the first few seconds of your content, tells people what to expect.

b) Steps: Steps are actions that occur *in order* and accomplish a goal when completed. Provided the early steps were clear and valuable, the person will want to know how to do them all to accomplish the overall goal.

Here's the difference between steps and lists. Steps are *actions* that must be done in a *specific order* to get a result. Lists can have just about anything on them in any order you want.

c) Stories: Stories describe events, real or imaginary. And stories worth telling often have some lesson or takeaway for the listener. You can tell stories about things that *have happened, might happen*, or *will never happen*. All three drive curiosity because people want to know what happens next.

You can use lists, steps, and stories on their own or interweave them. For example, you can have lists within steps, and a story about each list item.

> **Exercise #18: Pick one of the stories from Exercise #15. Outline the major points in the story or lessons you learned from it. Feel free to add mini stories for each lesson.**

3) Reward

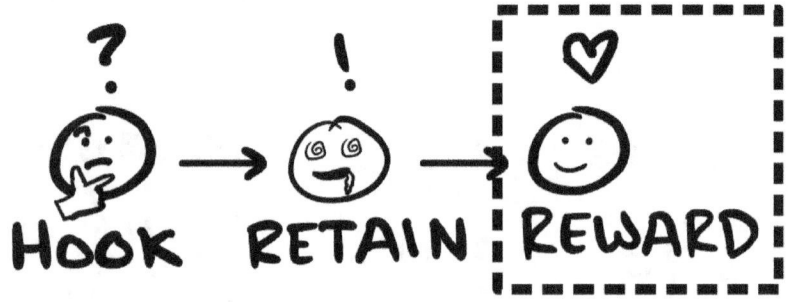

<u>How good your content is depends on how often it rewards your audience in the time it takes them to consume it.</u> Think *value per second*. So there is no such thing as too long, only *too boring*.

We can increase the chance reward happens by:

- Hooking the *right* audience with proper topics, headlines, and formatting

- Retaining them with lists, steps, and stories to get them curious and wanting more

- Clearly satisfying the reason the content hooked them to begin with.

Example: If your hook promises "7 Ways to Make Up with Your Spouse" and you give:

(A) four ways (B) seven ways that stunk (or they've heard them all before). (C) you're talking to a room of single guys who don't have spouses, *you did a bad job of rewarding them.* People will not want to watch again, and certainly won't share it.

<u>Bottom line:</u> Rewarding your audience means *matching or exceeding their expectations when they decide to consume your content.* Here's how you know if you succeeded: *your audience grows*. If it's not growing, your stuff isn't that good. Make more and you'll get better.

> **Exercise #19: Use the same story as Exercise #18. Doublecheck that you satisfied the promise of your headline. Write out what they can now <u>do</u> as a result of the content.**

So what's the difference between short and long form content? Answer: not much.

If you recall from earlier, the smallest amount of material it takes to hook, retain and reward attention is a **content unit**. So to create a longer piece of content, we simply link content units together.

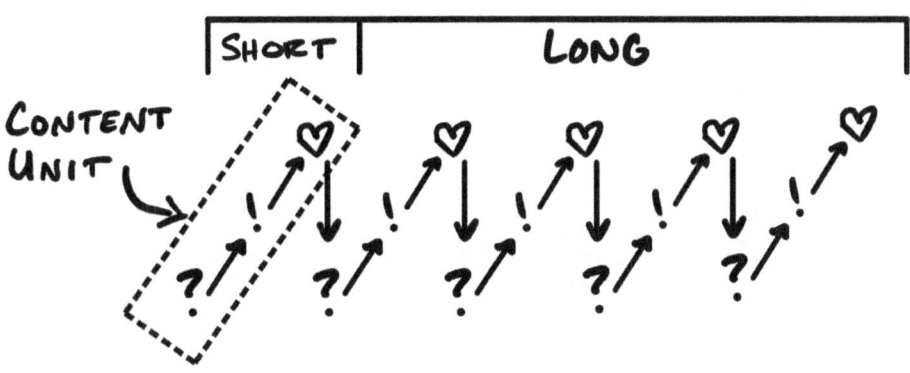

Start small, then build from there. Even if you start with longer content, which is fine, I suggest starting with shorter versions. You'll have an easier go of it.

Pro Tip: Make All Your Content For Strangers:

This is important. If you want to *grow* your warm audience, then you need to make content assuming the people consuming it have never heard of you before. If you make it for strangers then strangers will like it because… *you made it for them.* And they'll share it. And your audience will grow that much faster. Don't worry about repeating yourself. Your audience will appreciate the reminders.

Once you understand how to make a content unit, all you have to do is *more.* Then, your audience will grow. And once your audience grows big enough, you'll want to monetize it. And that's what's next.

#2 Post Free Content Part II

Monetize Your Audience

"Give-give-give, give-give-give, until they ask"

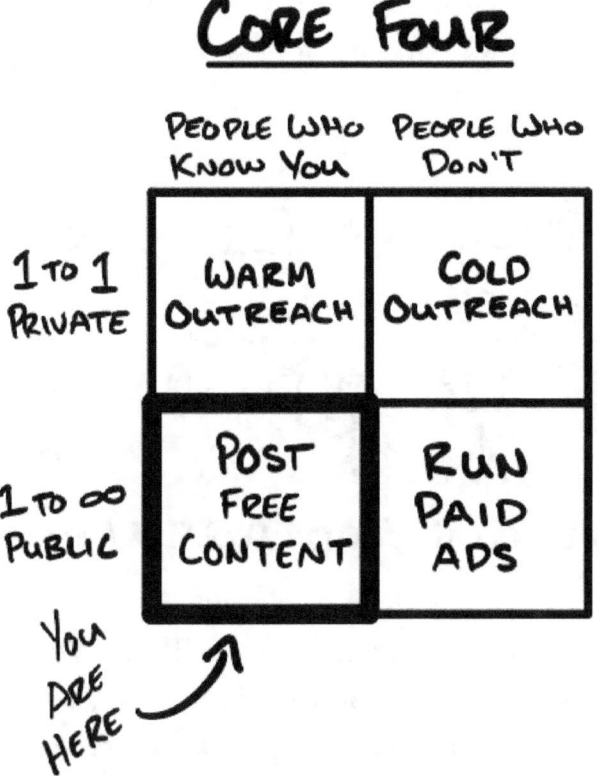

The point of this chapter is to show you how to monetize your warm audience.

First, we talk about how we can make offers and not be a spam monster - mastering the give : ask ratio.

Then, we'll talk about the two offer strategies to monetize the audience.

After that, I'll talk about how to scale your output so you can grow a bigger audience faster and make even more money.

Then, I'll share a bunch of lessons I've learned in building my own audience that I wish I had known sooner.

Finally, I'll wrap this up with how you can take action on everything *today*.

Mastering the Give: Ask ratio

Give more than you ask. The appropriate ratio has been studied. You need to give *at least 3.5 to 4x more than you ask*. This maintains an audience. If you want to grow faster, give far more than four times to every ask (think 10x-20x more). If you want to shrink your audience, ask more than you give.

And now that I have some experience with it, I've got a slight tweak on the traditional give-ask strategy that puts it on steroids: *Give until they ask.*

It's simple. If you give enough, *people start asking you*. They'll go to your website, DM you, email you, etc., to ask for more. When you use this strategy, you *give in public, ask in private*. And best of all, if you advertise this way, *your growth never slows*. You let the audience self-select when they're ready to give you money.

Bottom Line: The moment you start asking for money is the moment you decide to slow down your growth. So the more patient you are, the more you will get when you finally make your ask.

Action Step: Give give give give give *until they ask*

How To Make Money From Content: Ask

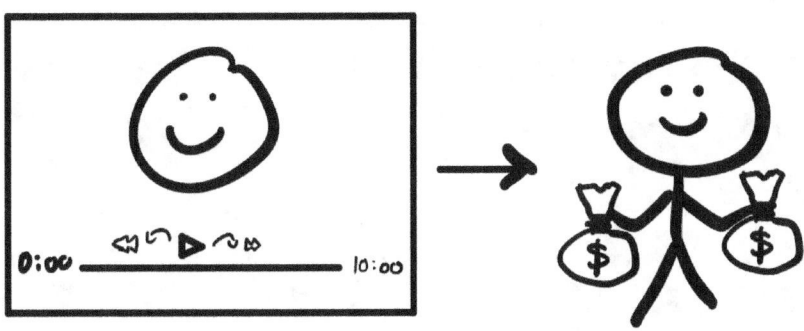

Sometimes you gotta ask. Think of 'asks' as commercials. You *interrupt this program with a very important message*. Since you are the one providing the value, you interrupt your own content with commercials about the stuff you sell. You pay the cost of potential loss of trust, slowing growth, and of course, the time it took you to gather the audience in the first place. And you get money in return. Now, I use two strategies to weave promotions into content: integrated offers and intermittent offers. Let's cover both.

INTEGRATED

SINGLE PIECE OF CONTENT

Integrated: You can advertise in every piece of content so long as you keep your give : ask ratio high. You will continue to grow your warm audience *and* get engaged leads. Win-win.

For example, if I make an hour-long podcast, having 3 x 30-second ads means I'd have 58.5 min of giving to 1.5 min of asking. Well above the 3:1 ratio.

I most commonly integrate the 'asks' - aka - CTAs after a valuable moment or the end of the content piece. Consider trying one of those places first - and make sure your audience growth doesn't slow. Then add in the second and so forth.

INTERMITTENT

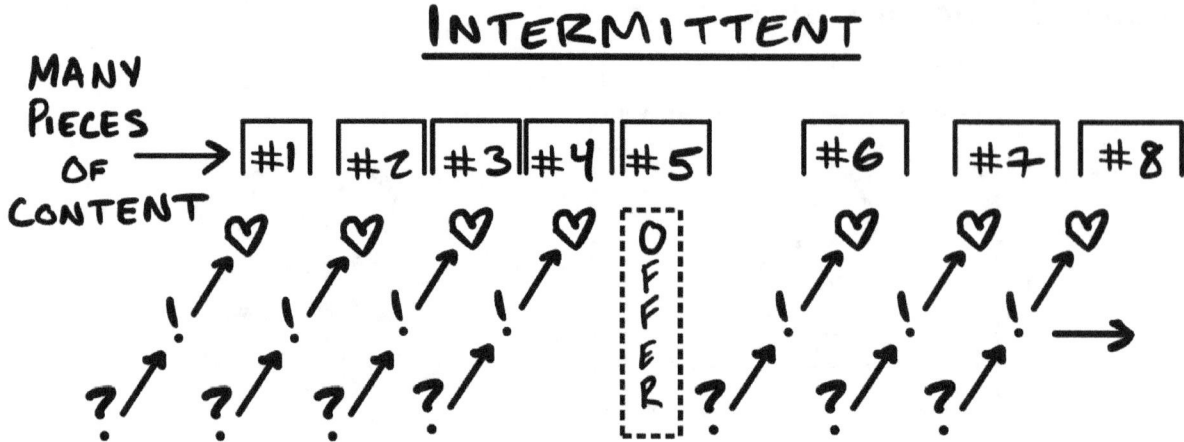

Intermittent: The second way you can monetize is through intermittent asks. Here's how it works. You make many pieces of content of pure 'gives' then occasionally make an 'ask' piece. Example: You make 10 'give' posts, and on the 11th, you promote your stuff.

The difference between the first way and the second way depends on the platform. On short platforms, the intermittent way will dominate. On long-form platforms, integrations are often your best bet.

Exercise #20: Add in the CTA from Exercise #7 from lead magnets or your core offer. Put a sentence before the CTA that links the CTA to this piece of content so it flows.

Author Note: If you need more help with offer creation, I wrote an entire book on it called *$100M Offers*. It also has a workbook and summary. You can check it out wherever you buy or read books.

How to Scale It

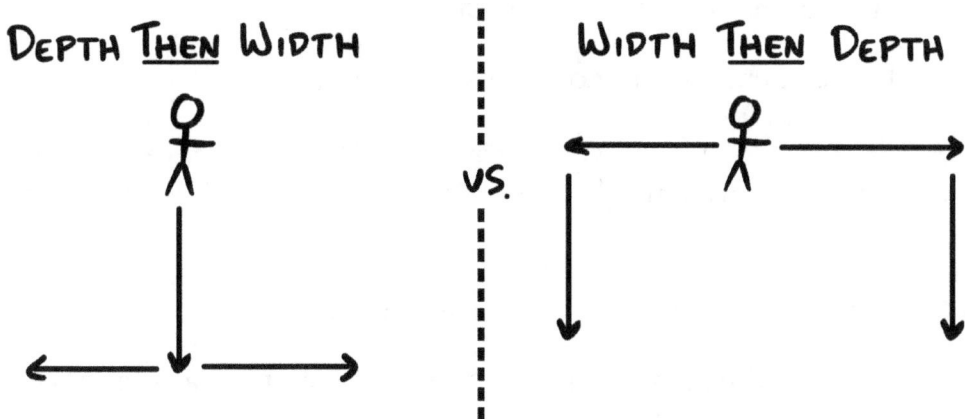

There are two opposing strategies to scale your warm audience. They both follow progressive steps. First, you have the depth-then-width approach. Then, you have the width-then-depth approach. Both are right. Here's how they work:

Depth then width: Maximize a platform, then move onto the next platform.

> Step #1: Post content on a relevant platform.

> Step #2: Post content regularly on that platform.

> Step #3: Maximize quality and quantity of the content on that platform. Short form, you may sometimes be able to get up to ten times per day per platform. Long form, you may have to get up to five days per week (see soap operas).

> Step #4: Add another platform while maintaining the quality and quantity on the first platform.

> Step #5: Repeat steps 1-4 until all relevant platforms are maximized.

Advantages: Once you figure out one platform, you maximize your return on that effort. Audiences compound faster the more you do. You take advantage of this compounding. Fewer resources are required to make this work.

Disadvantages: You have less low hanging fruit of new platforms and new audiences. You don't accomplish the feeling of 'omnipresence.' In the beginning, you risk your business being reliant on a single channel. This is a risk because platforms change all the time and sometimes ban you for no reason. If you only have one way to get customers, it can kill your business if it gets shut down.

Width then depth: Get on every platform early, then maximize them together.

Step #1: Post content on a relevant platform.

Step #2: Post content regularly on that platform.

Step #3: *Here's where this strategy differs from the one before.* Instead of maximizing your first platform. Move onto the next relevant platform while maintaining the previous.

Step #4: Continue until you are on all relevant platforms.

Step #5: Now, maximize your content creation on all platforms at once.

Advantages: You reach a broader audience faster. And, you can "repurpose" your content. So with a little extra work, you can capture tons of efficiency. With minimal changes to the format, you can make the same content fit multiple platforms. For example, it takes little extra effort to format a single short video across all platforms distributing short video content.

Disadvantages: It costs more labor, attention, and time, to do this well. Oftentimes, people end up with lots of bad content everywhere.

> **Exercise #21: Pick an approach**. Start posting. Then, go up the scaling steps over time.

7 Lessons I've Learned From Making Content

1) **Switch from "How to" to "How I." From "This is the best way" to "These are my favorite ways" etc.** (especially when starting out). Talk about what you've done, not what others should do. What you like, not this is *the* best.

2) **We Need To Be Reminded More Than We Need To Be Taught:** Keep repeating yourself. You'll get bored of your content before your whole audience even sees it.

3) **Narrow the focus of your content.** Just talk about what you know and have experience in. If you make educational content about stuff that you are not an expert in, you will look bad. Only teach what you know. Don't pretend.

4) **Content Creates Tools For Salespeople.** Create a master list of your "greatest hits." Label each 'hit' with the common concern it resolves for your prospects. Then, your sales team can send it before or after sales calls and help people decide to buy.

5) **Free Content Retains Paying Customers.** Somebody who buys your stuff is *more likely* to consume your free content. If your free content is valuable, your paying customers will like you more and stay loyal to your business longer. Free value strengthens their *perceived* ROI from your paid thing.

6) **People don't have shorter attention spans, they have higher standards.** Repeated for emphasis: *there's no such thing as too long, only too boring.*

7) **Avoid Pre-Scheduling Posts**. The posts I manually post perform better than ones I pre-schedule. So, I strongly believe in someone pressing the 'submit' button because it gives that last bit of pressure to get it right. Try it.

Benchmarks - How Well Am I Doing?

If our audience grows, we did good. But if our audience grows fast, we did *gooder*. So I like to measure my audience size and speed of growth monthly.

Here's what I measure:

1) Total followers and reach - *How big?* Track follower and reach absolute growth.

2) Rate of getting followers and reach - *How fast?* Track growth rate.

Alex Hormozi ✔
@AlexHormozi

It's amazing what you can accomplish if you don't stop once you start.

Your First Post

You've probably been providing value to other humans knowingly or unknowingly for a while. So the first post you make, *you can make an ask.* My hope is that it gets you your first engaged lead. Here was mine.

Alex Hormozi ✓
April 9, 2013 · Baltimore, MD · 🌐

Everyone,

For those of you who know me, you know two things:

1) I am terrible with all things technological. For example, I just heard about spotify a few weeks ago, seriously.
2) I love training/nutrition and "fitness" more than, well, a whole lot.

So, today is sort of special because it marks a day when my love of training vanquished my fear of technology.

What do I mean?

For the better part of a year I have been taking part in a free personal training project with the idea that I would give away free personal training to anyone who was willing to give some of their $500-$1000 to a cause of their choice. This way, they wouldn't have to be motivated by the same thing as me, but be motivated to give to their cause and benefit themselves. When I first introduced the idea, I was happily surprised with the amount of positive support I received.

So, almost a year from my first client, I NOW HAVE A WEBSITE!! to formally show some of the transformations that have gone underway using my programming and as a formal means of contacting me about signing up.
I CURRENTLY HAVE A FEW SLOTS OPEN IN MY ROSTER, SO DROP ME A NOTE QUICKLY IF YOU ARE INTERESTED! THANKS SO MUCH!

Take a second to check out some of the ridiculous transformations in record. time. CHECK IT OUT

It's definitely not perfect. But done is better than nothing. Start.

Exercise #22: Make your first post.

Post Content Daily Checklist	
Who:	Yourself
What:	Value: Give give give until they ask
Where:	Any media platform
To Whom:	People who already follow you
When:	Every morning, 7 days a week
Why:	Build goodwill. Get engaged leads.
How:	Written, image, videos, audio posts
How Much:	100 min per day
How Many:	As many times as the platform shows it
How Long:	As long as it takes.

Next Up

First, we start with warm outreach. We reach out to every person we have permission to contact. Second, we post publicly about the successes and lessons we have from our first clients. We post testimonials. We provide value. Then occasionally ask. We commit to doing both of these activities every day.

With these two methods alone you can eventually build a six- or seven-figure business. But you may want to go faster. So we venture from warm audiences who know us, to cold audiences who don't. We begin *reaching out to strangers*. This begins the third step in our advertising journey: cold outreach.

FREE GIFT: Everything I've Learned From Posting Content

I had to cut a lot of material to make this book manageable. If you want to know the fast and easy way to make content that builds trust in an audience - go to Acquisition.com/ training/leads. And, if you needed another reason besides 'it'll make you money'....it won't cost you any. It's free. Enjoy. And as always, you can also scan the QR code below if you hate typing.

Free Goodwill

"He who said money can't buy happiness hasn't given enough away." — *Unknown*

People who give without expectation live longer, happier lives *and* make more money. So if we've got a shot at that during our time together, darn it, I'm gonna try.

To do that, I have a question for you…

Would you help someone you've never met if it cost you nothing, but you didn't get credit?

Who is this person you ask? They are like you. Or, at least, like you used to be. Less experienced, wanting to make a difference, and needing help, but not sure where to look.

Acquisition.com's mission is *to make business accessible to everyone*. Everything we do stems from that mission. And, the only way for us to accomplish that mission is by reaching… well…*everyone*.

This is where you come in. Most people do, in fact, judge a book by its cover (and its reviews). So here's my ask on behalf of a struggling entrepreneur you've never met:

Please help that entrepreneur by leaving this book a review.

Your gift costs no money and less than 60 seconds to make real, but can change a fellow entrepreneur's life *forever*. Your review could help…

….one more small businesses provide for their community.

….one more entrepreneur support their family.

….one more employee get meaningful work.

…one more client transform their life.

…one more dream come true.

To get that 'feel good' feeling and help this person for real, all you have to do is…. and it takes less than 60 seconds…leave a review.

If you are on audible - hit the three dots in the top right of your device, click rate & review, then leave a few sentences about the book with a star rating.

If you are reading on kindle or an e-reader - scroll to the bottom of the book, then swipe up and it will prompt a review for you.

If for some reason these changed- you can go to Amazon (or wherever you purchased this) and leave a review right on the book's page.

If you feel good about helping a faceless entrepreneur, you are my kind of people. Welcome to #mozination. You're one of us.

I'm that much more excited to help you get more leads than you can possibly imagine. You'll love the tactics I'm about to share in the coming chapters. Thank you from the bottom of my heart. Now, back to our regularly scheduled programming.

- Your biggest fan, Alex

PS - Fun fact: If you provide something of value to another person, it makes you more valuable to them. If you'd like goodwill straight from another entrepreneur - and you believe this book will help them - send this workbook their way.

Exercise #23: If you liked this workbook so far, please leave it a review.

#3 Cold Outreach

How To Reach Out To Strangers To Get Engaged Leads

"Quantity has a quality all of its own" — Napoleon Bonaparte

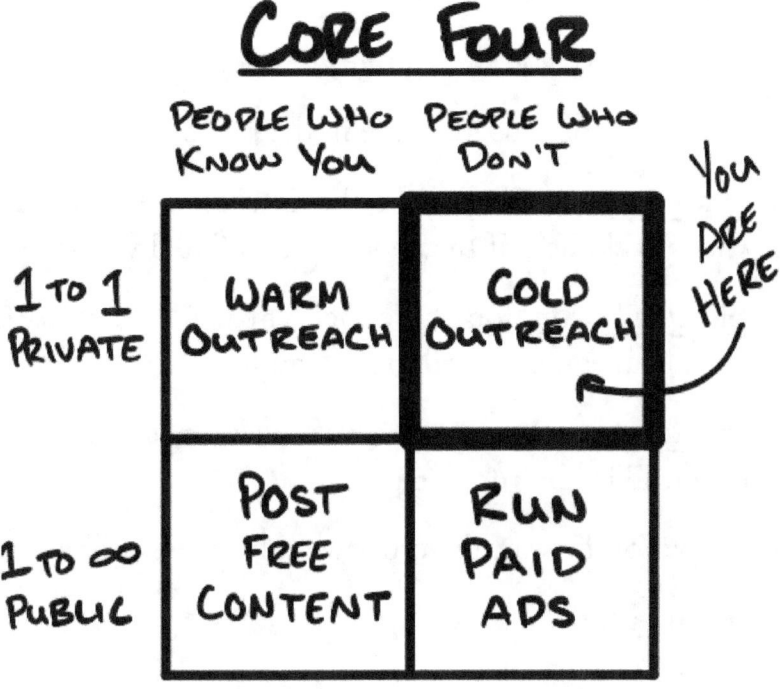

How Cold Outreach Works

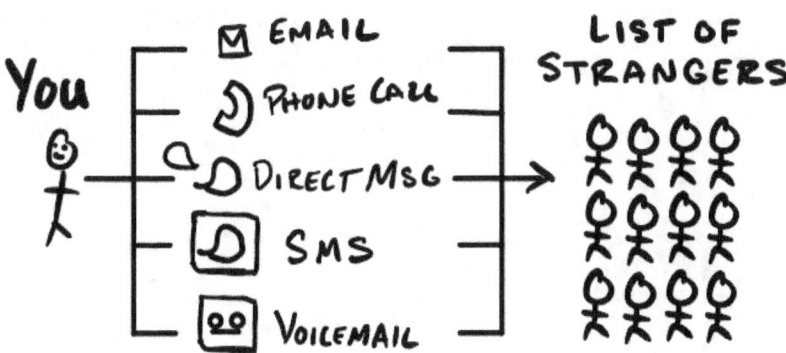

In this chapter, we focus on private one-to-one communication with cold outreach. For added context, cold outreach sits atop the foundation of warm outreach. So think of this as the more advanced cousin of warm outreach, no longer limited by your warm audience.

Cold outreach has one key difference from warm outreach: trust. Strangers don't trust you.

And compared to people who know us, strangers present <u>three</u> new problems.

1) First, you don't have a way to contact them. Duh.

2) Second, even if you can contact them, they ignore you.

3) Third, even if they give you their attention, they're not interested.

Let me describe what these problems look like in the real world.

<u>If you're knocking on doors</u>, you don't have the addresses. Then, even if you do, they don't open the door when you knock. If they open, they still tell you to pound sand.

<u>If you're sending cold emails</u>, you don't have their email addresses. Even if you do, they don't open the email. Even if they do, they don't respond.

<u>If you're sending direct messages</u>, you don't have a place to send it. Even if you do, they don't read it. Even if they read it, they don't reply.

Now that we got that out of the way, the order we solve these problems is:

1) Get a way to contact them

2) Figure out what to say

3) Contact them until they're ready and able to listen

<u>The Result</u>. We find lots of ways to contact the most qualified strangers. We reach out to a lot of them in a lot of ways a lot of times. Then, we overwhelm them with value upfront to get them to show enough interest to move forward.

Problem #1: "But how do I contact them?" →Build a List

With cold outreach, *we* get to pick our targets rather than them picking us. There are three different ways I get my targeted lead lists. First, I use software to scrape a list of names. Second, I pay brokers to assemble me a list of targeted leads. And if neither of those work, I manually scrape a list of names myself. Here's the process.

o <u>Step #1 Softwares</u>: I subscribe to as many softwares as I can that scrape leads from different sources. I search them all based on my criteria. The software then spits out names, job titles, contact information, etc. I try out a representative sample, say a few hundred from each software I use. Then, if the contact information is up to date, the leads are responsive, and they are the type of person the software claims them to be, bingo! Then I get as many leads as the software will give me. But if I can't seem to find the right audience, I move onto step two.

o <u>Step #2 Brokers</u>: I go to multiple list brokers and ask them to make me a list based on my audience criteria. They then send me a sample. I test out sample lists from each of the brokers. If I get good results from one or more brokers, I stick with their lists. And if I still can't find who I'm looking for, I move to step three.

o <u>Step #3 Elbow Grease</u>: I join groups and communities that I think have my audience. When I find people who meet my qualifications, I check to see if they have ways to contact them in the group's directory–like links to their social media profiles, etc. If they do, I add them to my list. If they don't, I can reach out to them within the platform hosting the group. I prefer to find contact information outside the group so I don't come off as someone solely trying to milk the group for business *but I will if I have to.*

In short, I work my way from the most accessible leads to the least accessible leads.

Exercise #24: Build your list. Find your scraping tool by searching "outbound leads scraping tool" or "database lead scraping." Find brokers the same way. With a few clicks, you'll find what you're looking for. Put your first 1000 names together. If you have more time than money, you might want to start at step three since it only costs time.

Pro Tip: Interest Groups Are The Warmest Cold Audience You Can Get

Interest groups contain the highest quality leads because they are concentrated pools of people looking for a solution. Give them one. Nowadays, there's software that can scrape information from these groups. Use it. They're one of my favorite places to fish.

Problem #2: "I have my list, but what do I say to them?" →Personalize, Then Give Big Fast Value

Now that you have your list of leads, you gotta figure out what to say. There are two important factors I emphasize to get strangers to engage: *personalization* and *big fast value*.

a) They Don't Know Us→Personalize (Act Like You Know Them). To get more leads to engage, we want the message to *look* like it's from someone they know. The best way to do that is to actually know something about the person you are contacting - aka - *personalization*. We want our *cold* reach out to look like a *warm* reach out.

Here's how. Get one to three pieces of information about the prospect. Then we want to complement them on it, and ideally, show them how it benefited us. People like people who like them. Even if someone doesn't know you, they'll give you more time if you know something about them. It might look like this…

…Imagine your phone rings from an unknown number and area code. Are you likely to pick it up? Probably not. What about if the number is from your area code? A little more likely. Why is that? Because *it might be someone you know*. So to take this concept further, imagine you pick up the phone…

…The person says "<Your name?>" then pausing (like a normal person). You'd say, "Yeah…who's this?" Now, if that person then went on to say, "It's Alex…*then pauses*…I watched a few of your videos and read that recent blog post you wrote on dog training. It was killer! Really helped me out with my Doberman. She's a beast! That peanut butter trick really helped. Thanks for that."

You could now take on the rest of the script because you bought yourself time.

Exercise #25: Do a little research on each lead before you reach out. We can do this ourselves, pay people to do it for us, or use software. Batch this work. Then, use your notes to figure out the first thing you'll open with to *feel more familiar.* <u>Note</u>: If you have deeper pockets, personalization technology exists. Just search online and you can find databases that also give you some relevant information you can use to talk to a lead.

Pro Tip: 50% Email Response Rate Bump

I took our cold outreach template and re-wrote it below a third grade reading level. The results: *50% more leads responded.* I now run all scripts and messages through a free reading level app online.

---

b) They Don't Trust Us→Big Fast Value. Strangers need a lot more incentive to move towards you than warm audience. So make your life easier by "giving away the farm." We're not trying to tickle their interest, <u>we're trying to blow their minds in under thirty seconds.</u>

You can directly make your offer, or offer a lead magnet, or both. It gives the person a strong reason to respond. If your offer/lead magnet isn't working for you, up the ante. Keep offering more until you *make it so good they feel stupid saying no.* They either buy from you or have nice things to say about you. Win-win.

Exercise #26: Clearly write down the big fast value you plan to provide each lead.

Problem #3: "I'm not getting enough chances to tell people about my amazing stuff, what do I do?" → Volume

Once we have our list of names, personal info, and our big sexy lead magnet, we need to get more strangers to see it. We do this in three ways. First, we automate delivery to the greatest extent possible. Next, we automate distribution to the greatest extent possible. Finally, we follow up more times in more ways.

a) Automated Delivery. To the extent that we can, automating delivery unlocks huge scale as someone doesn't need to literally communicate the message to the prospect. This means you get more engaged leads per unit of time (even if fewer engage by overall percentage). Here's what the difference between manual and automated delivery looks like.

Manual Examples: A live person can say a script to someone over the phone. You can send a personal voice memo to each lead. A person can write a handwritten letter to every person on the list. If it takes a person time to convey the message each time, it's manual.

Automated Examples: We can send a pre-recorded voice memo to someone's direct messages. We can send a pre-recorded voicemail to someone's voicemail box. We can send templated emails to an inbox or a templated text to someone's phone. We can send a pre-recorded video. Etc. You record your message one time and then send the same message to everyone.

b) Automate Distribution. Once we have our messages prepared, we gotta distribute them.

MANUAL   vs.   AUTOMATED

Manual examples: Dial each phone number. Click send on each email, direct message, text, etc.

Automated examples: Use a robot to dial multiple numbers at a time. Send a blast of 1000 emails, texts, voicemails at one time. Etc.

Generally speaking, you sacrifice personalization for scale. You get a higher response rate with personalized messages. *The fewer leads you have, the less automation you should use.*

Exercise #27: Search for tools that can automate portions of your work. Ex: if you make phone calls five days per week, try out a new dialer or tech one of the days and see how it does compared to your standard dialer.

c) Follow up. More times. More ways. There are two more ways you can get more from your list of names.

LEADS LIST

NAME... 555-5555
NAME... 555-5555
NAME... 555-5555
NAME... 555-5555
NAME... 555-5555
NAME... 555-5555
NAME... 555-5555

TODAY x3...
TOMORROW...
NEXT DAY...

First, you try to contact them more than once. Second, use more than one way to contact them. The more ways and more times you try to contact someone, the more likely you are to contact them. People respond to different methods. For example, I never respond to phone calls. But, I reply to direct messages far more.

I like to email first. You know why? Because most people don't respond. If someone doesn't respond to one of your reach out methods, use that as a reason to follow up with another method. *"Hey I'm calling you to follow up about my email."* We either get a response or a real reason to reach out again. We win either way.

And once you do get them booked for an appointment, expect more than one conversation. Remember, we're contacting complete strangers. Outreach takes more touch points with people who don't know you. So expect two to three conversations before a higher ticket sale. Shoot for less, but expect more when you start out.

Bottom line: Act like you're *actually* trying to get ahold of these people, rather than going through the motions, and you probably will.

Exercise #28: Contact each lead multiple times in multiple ways.

Next, once you finish contacting your list, start back at the top again. This actually works for three reasons. One, because they simply may not have seen your first series of messages. Two, even if they do see it, it may not have been a good moment to respond. Three, their circumstances may have changed. They might not have needed you then, but need you desperately now. So try again in three to six months and get an entirely new group of engaged leads *from the same list*.

Exercise #29: Set a reminder for three to six months. Then, reach out again. Tip: If you're new to an outreach team, shadow the best guy on the team and do twice their volume of reach outs. You'll get better in half the time.

Three Problems Strangers Create→Solved

I wrote the book in this order to build on itself. Start with warm reach outs. Get some reps. Post some content to grow your warm audience. Get even more reps. Then, you'll be ready for cold reach outs.

And now, we solved the three core problems cold audiences create: finding the right list of people, getting them to pay attention to you, and getting them to engage. Victory!

Benchmarks–How well am I doing?

It just comes down to what you make versus what you spend in labor to make it. To calculate our return on advertising, we add up all labor and software costs associated with steps one through three in the section before last.

Let's imagine we have a team doing cold calls:

- We pay them $15 per hour and $50 per shown appointment or "shows."

- We make $3600 in profit per sale.

- Leads cost us ten cents.

- They call 200 leads per day.

- We would likely get about two shows per day from one rep.

- If they worked eight hours per day, we would pay $120 in labor and $100 in show commissions per rep and $20 for the leads.

- This means we would pay $240 for two shows or $120 per show.

- If we closed 33% of shows, our cost to get a client (excluding commissions) would be $360.

- Since we get $3600 profit per new client, we would make a 10:1 return.

The rule of thumb in business is you want to be above 3:1 return. Personally, I shoot for much higher, because I like to make more money. So, that's how cold outreach works. Then, you just add more employees. Which, if you do have employees, give them a fixed number of leads to work each. This way you can hold them to quotas. Just something that's worked well for me.

This Sounds Hard, Why Bother?

Most people dramatically underestimate the amount of volume it takes to use cold outreach. They also underestimate how long it takes. But there are seven *enormous* benefits to using cold outreach:

1) <u>You don't need to create lots of content or ads.</u>

2) <u>Your competition won't know what you're doing because everything is private.</u>

3) <u>It's incredibly reliable.</u>

4) <u>Fewer platform changes.</u> Public platforms change all the time, but private communication rarely do.

5) <u>Compliance is less painful.</u>

6) <u>No spokesperson = Sellable business.</u> It doesn't require your face to work.

7) <u>Hard for your competitors to copy the size of a massive team.</u>

Your Turn

If you recall our advertising checklist this kicks off your journey to get more engaged leads with cold outreach. You start this as you run out of people to advertise to, or, because you just want more. Here's a sample.

Cold Reach Outs Daily Checklist	
Who:	Yourself
What:	Hook + Lead Magnet/ Core Offer
Where:	Any private communication platform
To Whom:	List: Scraped, bought, or software used.
When:	Every morning, 7 days a week
Why:	Get leads to engage to sell stuff
How:	Live calls, voicemail drops, email blasts, text How: blasts, direct message texts, video messages, voice messages, direct mail pieces, hand written cards, etc.
How Much:	100 Per Day
How Many:	Day 1 - 2x, Day 2 - 2x, Day 7 - 1x
How Long:	As long as it takes.

Pro Tip: Count in 100s

This is a volume game. You will need to do a lot of volume, efficiently, to get the results you want. Don't set a daily goal below 100. And don't stop for 100 days minimum. If you do 100 reach outs for 100 days straight, I promise you will start getting new engaged leads.

Next Up

Now that you have set your commitment for this cold outreach method, we move onto the last thing a single person can do to advertise: run paid ads.

FREE GIFT: Cold Outreach Script Samples

I had to cut scripts to make this book a manageable length. If you want to model your scripts off them, go to: Acquisition.com/training/leads. And, if you needed another reason besides 'it'll make you money'....it won't cost you any. It's free. Enjoy. And as always, you can also scan the QR code below if you hate typing.

81

#4 Run Paid Ads Part I: Making An Ad

How To Publicly Advertise to Strangers

Advertising is the only casino where, with enough skill, you become the house.

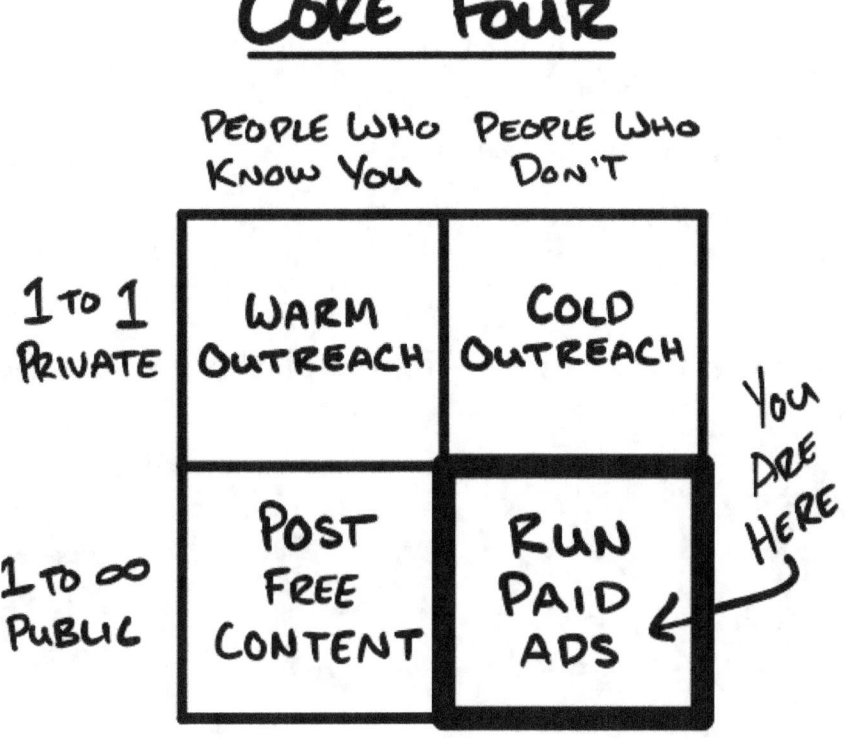

How Paid Ads Work

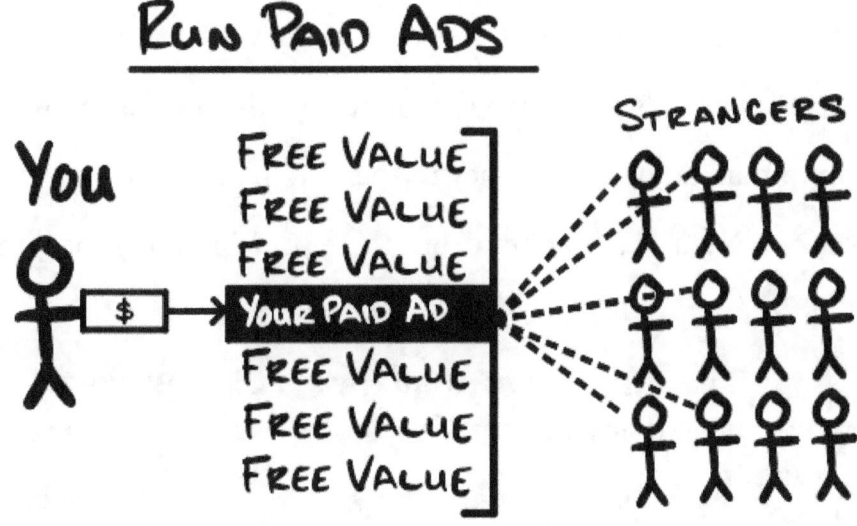

Paid ads offer a fast way to reach cold audiences at scale by paying to access another business's audience. While riskier than other methods, paid ads can generate more leads when done right. Unlike the other methods, your reach is guaranteed. The hard part lies in efficiency - balancing how much you spend against how much you get back.

Paid ads give us four new problems to solve. Let's break them down together:

1) Knowing where to advertise

2) Getting the right audience to see it

3) Making the best ad for them to see

4) Getting permission to contact them

Step 1: "But where do I advertise?" → Find a platform where these four things are true

Platforms distribute content to an audience. And wherever there's an audience, you can usually advertise. Here's what I look for in a platform I want to advertise on:

• I've used it and gotten value from it as a consumer. So I have some idea how it works.

• I can target people on the platform interested in my stuff.

• I know how to format ads specific to the platform (which I'll dive into in step three).

• I have the minimum amount of money to spend to place an ad.

...And yes, platforms change all the time, but these principles stay the same.

Exercise #30: Pick a platform that meets all four requirements. Start consuming the ads on that platform. If you're not sure, start on the platform your competitors use most.

Step #2: "But how do I get the right people to see it?" → Target them

You find the right people by first picking the right platform. Next, you try and get the highest number of people you think will buy your stuff to see your ad. So, we do the second round *within* the platform itself. Modern advertising platforms have two ways to target. You can use them separately or combine them:

1) <u>Target a lookalike audience.</u> Lookalike audiences are a targeting tool on modern ad platforms. You provide a list of contacts, and the platform finds similar users to show your ads to. To do it: Upload a list of current and previous customers. Add warm contacts and cold leads to reach the minimum if necessary.

2) <u>Target with factors of your choosing.</u> Targeting options include: age, income, gender, interests, time, location, etc. Basic filters on top of the platform-generated lookalike audience are a simple way to get more of the right people to see your ads. End result: more efficient ads.

Pro Tip: Local Targeting

Since local markets are already *tiny* in comparison to national markets, you won't want to add many more filters. Be as specific as possible, but no further. The local market on its own is already .1% of a nation, so you're already pretty narrow.

The more filters you use, the more specific the list. The more specific the list, the more efficient your ads but the faster you will "burn" through it. However, this specificity sets you up to get more wins early on. The wins from smaller specific audiences now give you the money to advertise to larger and broader audiences later. *This is how you scale.*

> **Exercise #31: Create an audience to target.**

Step #3 "But what should my ad say?" → Call Out + Value + Call to Action (CTA)

My best ads have three elements.

1) Call Outs - I need to get prospects to notice my ad

2) Value - I need to get them interested in what I have to offer

3) Calls to Action - I need to tell them what to do next

1) Call Out: *People noticing your ad is the most important part of the ad...by a lot.*

Imagine you're at a cocktail party in a big ballroom. Lots of people talking in groups. Loud music playing in the background. In all that noise, a single sound pierces through it all and you turn around. Wanna know the sound? Your name. You hear it, and *instantly* look for the source.

A **callout** *is whatever you do to get the attention of your audience.* Call outs go from hyper-specific - to get one person's attention - to not at all specific - to get everyone's attention. Let me explain. If someone drops a tray of dishes, *everyone* looks. If a child yells "MOM!", then the *moms* look. If someone says your name, only *you* look. But again, they all get attention. And I try to make my call outs specific enough to get the right people *and* broad enough to get as many of them as I can. So pay close attention to how advertisers use call outs, especially the ones targeting your audience.

Here's what I look for with verbal callouts- *using words to get attention:*

1) <u>Labels</u>: A word or set of words putting people into a *group*. These include features, traits, titles, places, and other descriptors. Ex: *Clark County Moms* *Gym Owners* *Remote Workers* *I'm looking for XYZ* etc. To be most effective, *your ideal customers need to identify with the label.*

2) <u>Yes-Questions</u>: Questions where if people answer "yes, that's me" they qualify themselves for the offer. Ex: *Do you wake up to pee more than once a night?* *Do you have trouble tying your shoes?* *Do you have a home worth over $400,000?*

3) <u>If-Then Statements</u>: *If* they meet your conditions *then* you help them make a decision. *If you run over $100,000 per month in ads, we can save you 20% or more... *If you were born between 1978 and 1986 in Muskogee Oklahoma, you may qualify for a class action lawsuit…*If you want to XYZ, then pay attention…*

4) <u>Ridiculous Results</u>: Bizarre, rare, or out of the ordinary stuff someone would want. *Massage studio books out two years in advance. Clients furious.* *This woman lost 50 pounds eating pizza and fired her trainer* *The government is handing out thousand dollar checks to anyone who can answer three questions* Etc.

Callouts don't have to be just words. They can also be noises or visuals in the environment. Let's go back to the cocktail party. Sure, a dropped tray of dishes would get everyone's attention, but so would the cling*cling*cling* of a knife against a champagne flute. They both get everyone's attention for different reasons–one signals an embarrassing disaster and the other signals important news… *but, in either case, everyone still wants to know what happens next.* <u>So if the platform allows, good advertisers use verbal and nonverbal callouts together.</u>

Here's what I look for with nonverbal callouts- *using the setting and spokesperson to get attention:*

1) <u>Contrast</u>: Any stuff that "sticks out" in the first few seconds. The colors. The sounds. The movements etc. Note what catches your attention.

2) <u>Likeness</u>: Think visually *showing* labels–features, traits, titles, places, and other descriptors that people identify with. People want to work with people who look, talk, and act in ways familiar to them (and you may not look, talk, or act in ways familiar to them). So if you serve a broad customer base use more ethnicities, ages, genders, personalities, etc. in your ads. If you serve a narrow customer base (ex: medical devices for seniors), then use people who look like them.

3) <u>The Scene</u>: Think *showing* the Yes-Questions and If-Then statements. Ex: An ad with a person tossing and turning in bed calls out people with sleep troubles.

Exercise #32: Record ten or so new ads every week. But, record thirty or more first sentences or questions to begin the ad. With thirty callouts and ten main ads you can make three hundred variations in a matter of hours. Once you know the best callout, you apply it to all ads.

2) Get Them Interested. Make the benefits look as big as possible and the costs look as small as possible. This makes an offer or lead magnet as valuable as it can be and gets the most engaged leads because of it. Clearly answer: *why should I be interested in your thing?* I use the What Who When Framework.

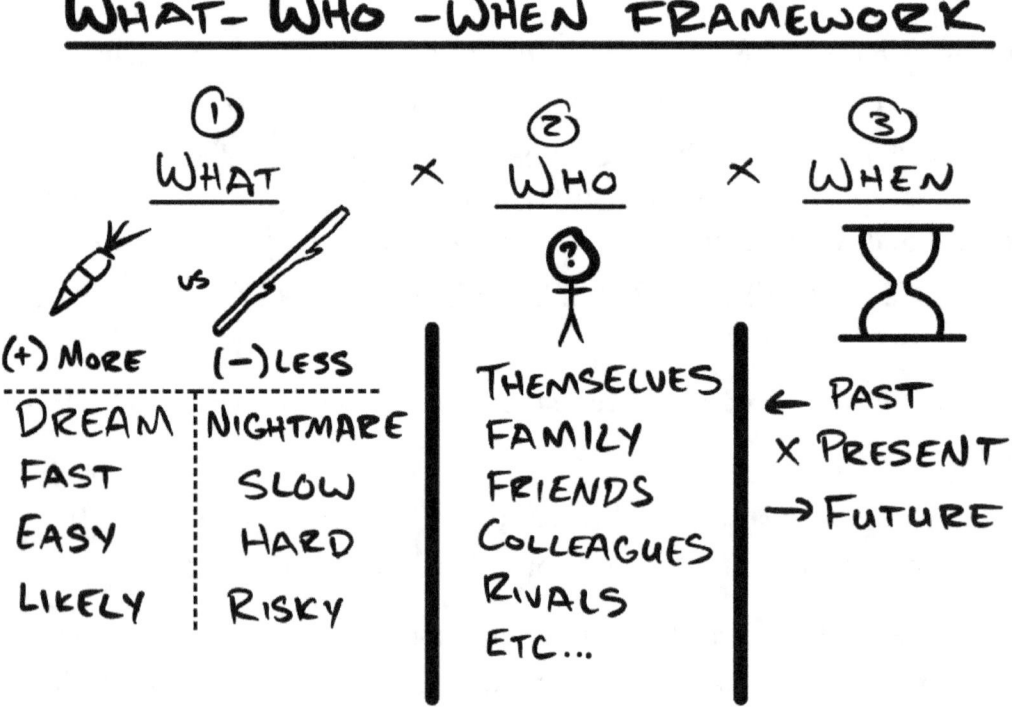

So let's start with The What: Eight Key Elements

- **Dream Outcome:** Show the maximum benefit achievable with your product/service.

- **Opposite (Nightmare):** Highlight the pain of going without your solution.

- **Perceived Likelihood of Achievement:** Lower perceived risk of failure.

- **Opposite (Risk):** Emphasize the risk of not acting.

- **Time Delay:** Demonstrate the slow progress or stagnation without your solution.

- **Opposite (Speed):** Show how much faster they'll achieve goals with your offering.

- **Effort and Sacrifice:** Illustrate the work and skill required without your solution.

- **Opposite (Ease):** Demonstrate how your solution reduces effort and preserves what they love.

Those are the 8 key elements that address the prospect's desires, fears, and perceptions about achieving their goals, positioning your product or service as the ideal solution. Now we fully understand The What – how we deliver the four value elements, and how we avoid their four opposites. We now go to the next W - The Who.

Who: Humans are status-driven, with status determined by how others treat them. Good ads show how the product/service changes how others treat the customer. Two key groups to consider: Customers gaining status - *and* - the people giving status (spouse, kids, family, colleagues, bosses, friends, rivals). Multiple perspectives offer multiple ways to demonstrate status improvement. This gives us more ways to show benefits beyond the customer's direct experience.

Examples:

- For weight loss: kids' new role model, spouse's health improvement, career advancement.
- For business: spouse's reduced nagging, kids noticing less stress, competitors' awareness

Applying each WHO perspective to each WHAT value driver to create loads of stories and angles. That leads me to the third lens of the What-Who-When framework - The When.

When: The "When" element in ad creation focuses on expanding the prospect's perspective across their timeline:

1. Consider past, present, and future consequences of decisions

2. Visualize scenarios from both the prospect's and others' perspectives

3. Highlight negative outcomes to avoid without the product/service

4. Contrast with positive outcomes if they buy

5. Combine "towards good" and "away from bad" motivators

Use this timeline approach to create better and more varied angles in your ads to find the message that best resonates with your prospect.

Putting the What, the Who, and the When together, we answer *WHY they should be interested.*

When we combine:

- everything we can to get the prospect going *toward* the four value drivers, while also getting them *away from* their opposites

- the many perspectives we can show them gaining status, *and*

- different timelines for each…

…This adds up to *why* they should be interested. Now, we have a lot of ways to get them interested! And - the more angles we cover, the more interested they'll become.

> **Pro Tip: Get Unlimited Inspiration.**
>
> Many platforms have a database of ads past and present. As of this moment, if you search "[PLATFORM] ad library" in a search engine, in a few clicks you will find them. If you see an ad that runs for a long time (a month or more), assume it's profitable. Then, take notes on the callouts they use, how they illustrate the value elements, and their CTAs. Look for <u>the words they use</u> *and* <u>how they demonstrate them</u>. Break down fifty or so ads and you will have a massive head start to creating winners of your own.

Exercise #33: Search the ad library on any platform to break down 50 or more of your competitors' ads and identify the What, Who, and When. Model those in your first ads.

3) CTA - Tell Them What To Do Next

If your ad got them interested, then your audience will have huge motivation… for a tiny time. Take advantage. <u>Tell them exactly what to do next</u>. <u>Make CTAs quick and easy</u>. Easy phone numbers, obvious buttons, simple websites.

Step #4 "How do I get their info?" → Get Permission To Contact Them

After they take the action–Get. Their. Contact. Information. My favorite way to get contact information is a simple landing page. Here are my three favorite templates. Pick one and start testing.

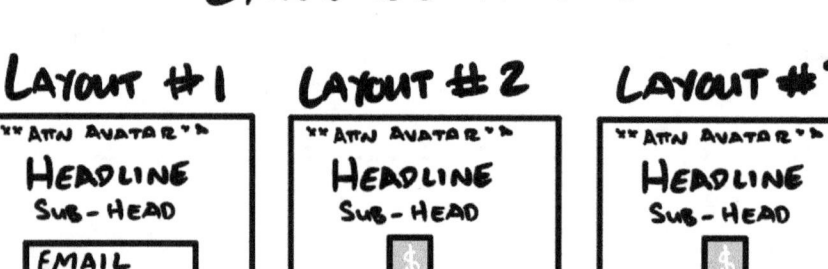

And make your landing pages match your ads in every way possible. You want a continuous experience from "click to close."

Get more people through more steps by reminding them of the action they just took. And show how taking the next action aligns with it, you'll get more people to take the second action (Contact Info).

> **Exercise #34: Build your first landing page.** Build a landing page or pay someone to do it for you. It takes 10 minutes or $200. Pay with whichever you value least. **Now, run your ad.**

In the next chapter we break down how well we did and how to adjust.

#4 Run Paid Ads Part II: Money Stuff

"I'm just trying to buy a dolla' and sell it for two" — *Proposition Joe, The Wire*

All advertising works. The only thing that differs between advertisements is how *well* they work. It's all about *the return on your investment.* And with paid ads it gets clear as day because you put X dollars in for people to see the ad and get Y dollars out if they buy your stuff.

This chapter answers four big questions about ads as I understand them:

- How much do I spend? →Three Phases of Scaling Ads

- How do I know how well I'm doing? →Cost & Benchmarks

- If my ads aren't profitable, how do I fix it? →Client Financed Acquisition.

- What do I wish I had known before I ran my first paid ad? →Lessons

"But how much do I spend on paid ads?"→ The Three Phases of Scaling Paid Ads

There are three stages to spending money on ads as I see it.

Phase One: Track Money. Before spending a dollar on ads, set everything up so you can accurately track your returns. Watch a tutorial on how to do it or pay someone. It's copy-paste.

Phase Two: Lose money (half-joking). It's investing in a money printing machine. You'll lose more times than you win, but when you win, you win big. Budget two times the 30-day customer cash when testing new ads. It costs money to build an advertising machine, but it's worth it long-term.

Phase Three: Print Money. When you're making more than you spend, the answer is simple - spend as much as you can. Reverse your budget from your sales goals. If the number terrifies you, you're doing it right. Trust the data. This is how you scale, and that's why most people never do.

"How well am I doing?" - Cost & Returns - Efficiency Benchmarks

Efficient paid ads make more money than they cost. I measure efficiency by comparing lifetime gross profit (LTGP) to cost to acquire a customer (CAC). LTGP is all the money a customer ever spends minus delivery costs. It's the actual money you use to run your business.

A good LTGP to CAC ratio is at least 3 to 1. Businesses struggling to scale often have ratios less than this.

Two big levers to improve LTGP:CAC:

1. Make CAC lower - Get cheaper customers through more efficient ads.

2. Make LTGP higher - Increase how much you make per customer with a better business model.

I prefer to do both for maximum money.

Often, entrepreneurs think they have crappy ads (high CAC) when they really have a crappy business model (Low LTGP). The difference between winners and losers is usually how much they make off each customer.

To know where to focus, use industry average CAC as a guide. If your CAC is below 3x industry average, focus on your business model. If it's above, focus on advertising.

Remember, costs can only approach zero, but how much you make can go up to infinity. Increasing ad efficiency beyond a certain point is like trying to "save your way" to a billion dollars.

"My ads aren't profitable, how do I fix it?" → Client Financed Acquisition

For many businesses, LTGP is bigger than CAC, but not after the first purchase. This cash flow problem cripples your ability to scale ads. But if your customer spends more than it costs to get and fulfill them in the first 30 days, you have client financed acquisition.

Example:

- $15/month membership, $5 to deliver = $10 gross profit/month

- Average member stays 10 months = $100 LTGP

- If CAC is $30, LTGP:CAC ratio is 3.3:1

Problem: You spent $30 in ads and only got $10 back initially.

Solution: Immediately sell more stuff

- $100 upsell (100% margins) that 1 in 5 customers take = $20 average upsell per customer

- This takes us from $10 to $30 in the first 30 days, breaking even

Now you can get another customer while collecting $10 profit/month for 9 more months. This is how you print money.

Bottom Line: Get customers to pay you back in the first 30 days so you can recycle cash to get more customers. It's how I've scaled *many* companies past $1M/mo in 12 months without outside funding.

Personal Lessons from Paid Ads

1. Don't Confuse Sales Problems With Advertising Problems: The cost to get customers doesn't only come from advertising. If engaged leads have the problem you solve and money to spend, but aren't buying, you have a sales problem, not an advertising problem.

2. Your Best Free Content Can Make The Best Paid Ads: Free content that generates sales or performs well often makes great paid ads. User Generated Content (UGC) like customer testimonials or reviews can be killer ads too. Have a system to encourage these public posts is an effortless way to get potential ads.

3. If You Say You Suck At Something, You Will Probably Suck At It: Never say "I'm not techy" or "I hate tech stuff." It just keeps you poorer. Saying this for years can waste time and money, but concentrated effort can reverse this quickly. "If this idiot can do it, so can I."

Your Turn

I can teach you how to place an ad in twenty minutes for $100. It's worth it because you'll learn that running ads is easier than you think. Platforms spend zillions to make it as simple as possible. Just search "HOW TO PLACE A [PLATFORM] AD" and spend $100 to place one. Start with an acceptable amount of money you're willing to lose each month, expecting to lose it while you're learning, not earning.

Paid Ads Daily Checklist	
Who:	Yourself
What:	Your Offer
Where:	Any platform/ audience you can buy access to
To Whom:	Target audience or lookalike audience
When:	Everyday, 7 days per week
Why:	Get engaged leads to sell
How:	Call Out + 3Ws + CTA
How Much:	Learning Budget, Then Reverse to Sales Goal
How Many:	30+ Call Outs x 10 Ads
How Long:	As long as it takes.

FREE GIFT: Bonus Training - Paid Ads Fast Track

Running paid ads is the fast track. It's high risk high reward. I recorded a deeper breakdown of paid ads frameworks that have served me across industries and price points. You can find it here for free, as always: Acquisition.com/training/leads. My gift to you - money you'll make in the future. And as always, you can also scan the QR code below if you hate typing.

Core Four On Steroids: More Better New

"If at first you don't succeed, use force."

How To Get Even More Leads: More Better New

What if you are doing the core four and still not getting as many engaged leads as you want? There are three ways to boost *any* of the core four to get even more engaged leads *on your own*: **More, Better, New**.

Simply stated:

1) You can do *more* of what you're currently doing.

2) You can do what you're currently doing *better*.

3) You can do it somewhere *new*.

So let's start with the one I actually do first: *More*.

More

The next obvious thing to get more engaged leads is to do *more* advertising. *A lot more.* Crank up the volume to your max capacity. Even with no improvements, doubling your inputs will get more engaged leads. The biggest increases often come from advertising *more*.

Here's how I do *more*: The Rule of 100. Do 100 primary actions every day, for 100 days in a row. If you do this, you will get more engaged leads. Commit to the rule of 100 and you will never go hungry again.

> ## Exercise #35: Do the rule of 100.
>
> ☐ Warm Reach Outs: 100 reach outs per day
> ☐ Post Content: 100 minutes per day making content
> ☐ Cold Reach Outs: 100 reach outs per day (use automation)
> ☐ Paid Ads: 100 minutes per day making ads, run for 100 days straight

Better

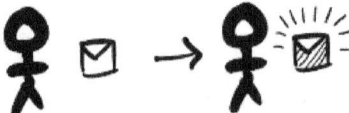

Getting better gets you more leads for the same effort. You can only get better by testing. Do more until it breaks, then make it better. Focus on the "constraint" - the step where the most leads drop off. If you're not sure, optimize advertising front to back. Improving the constraint gives the biggest boost in results.

Here's how I get better: I test one thing per week per platform. This way, you learn what worked, see how changes affect other steps, prioritize tests, and run them long enough to see improvements.

Exercise #36: Improve weekly.

☐ Look at results and pick winners for each platform test
☐ Log the results
☐ Come up with the next test
☐ If you can't beat the current version in four tries, move to the next constraint. Only when improvements bring diminishing returns do we try something *new*.

New

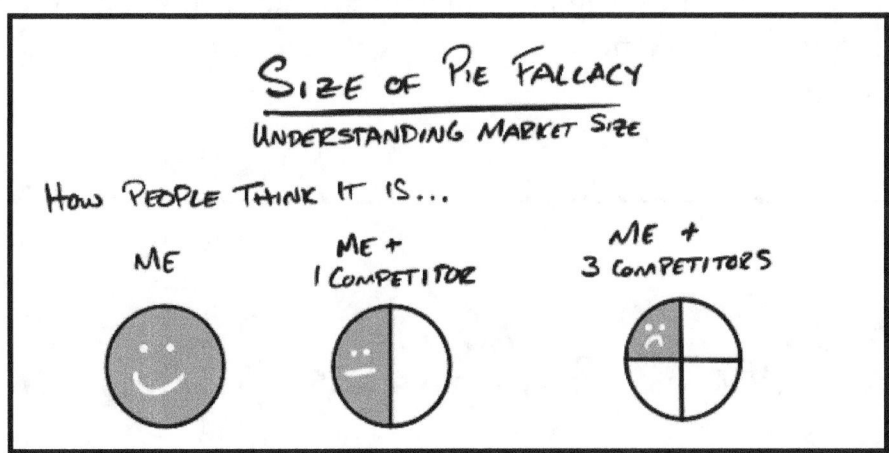

When to do new: When returns from doing more↔better are lower than what you could get from a new placement or way of advertising.

Most business owners look only at the platform and tiny community they market in. And usually, there are only three or four big companies marketing in their niche. So, they assume those companies *must* split the *entire* market between them. This is false. **The image below reflects reality.**

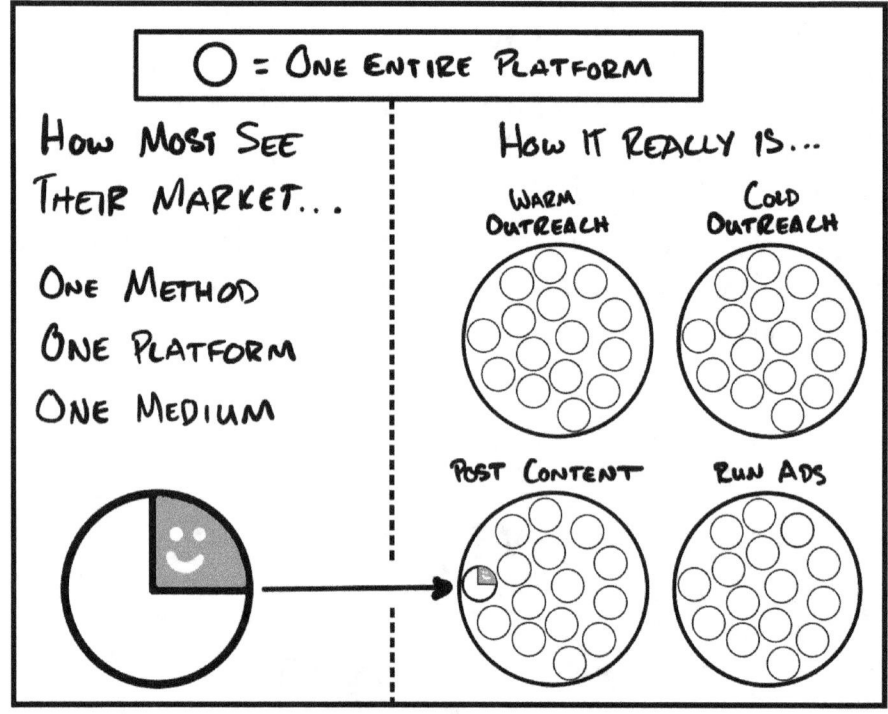

The Size Of The Pie Fallacy: Small businesses often mistakenly assume their tiny slice of advertising is the entire available market. This keeps them poorer than they should be.

There are many other slices of attention just inside the tiny universe of "post content." You can add new placements, new platforms, or new core four activities.

The order I pick my next 'new' comes down to one thing: what will get me the most leads for the amount of work? Nine times out of ten, it goes like this:

<u>New placements:</u> Ex: You switch from making Instagram story ads to messenger ads.

<u>New Platforms:</u> Ex: YouTube shorts to Instagram shorts.

<u>New Core Four:</u> Ex: You go from making content only, to adding in paid ads.

Bottom Line: No matter how you advertise, you could do it in new ways or places. Each gets us what we want - more leads.

Exhaust "more" and "better" first. Then try new in this order: new placement, new platform, new core four activity. Measure, scale up using more–better, then rinse and repeat.

Conclusion

Advertising is the *process of making known*. To get engaged leads, you have to tell strangers about your stuff. There are only four ways a *single* person can advertise, trading time, money, or both. You can advertise to people who know you (warm) or strangers (cold), publicly (content/ads) or privately (outreach).

After warm outreach, if you have more time than money, move to posting content. If you have more money than time, go with cold outreach or running ads. Just pick one, then max it out. Do more. Do better. Do new.

All advertising methods compound together. Every combination of the core four advertising activities boost each other in some way.

I've done 'em all, building various businesses using different combinations of these methods. There are many ways to get engaged leads. If you master one, you will be able to feed yourself for the rest of your life. They all work if you do.

Next Up

If you follow the steps in this book, you'll run out of hours in the day. You won't be able to do any more, any better… let alone add anything new! So you'll need help on your journey to the land of endless leads. You'll need allies. Those allies come in four different flavors. And since there are more of them than there are of you, they're the key to getting there. So let's go get them.

FREE GIFT: Bonus Training - More, Better, New

This is one of my favorite topics around scaling businesses. Our portfolio CEOs cite this as one of the most impactful frameworks I've given them. If you want to see a video version of me breaking this down . You can find it here for free, as always: Acquisition.com/training/leads. And as always, you can also scan the QR code below if you hatetyping.

SECTION IV:
GET LEAD GETTERS

Get people who get you more leads

"Give me a lever long enough and a fulcrum on which to place it, and I shall move the world." — Archimedes

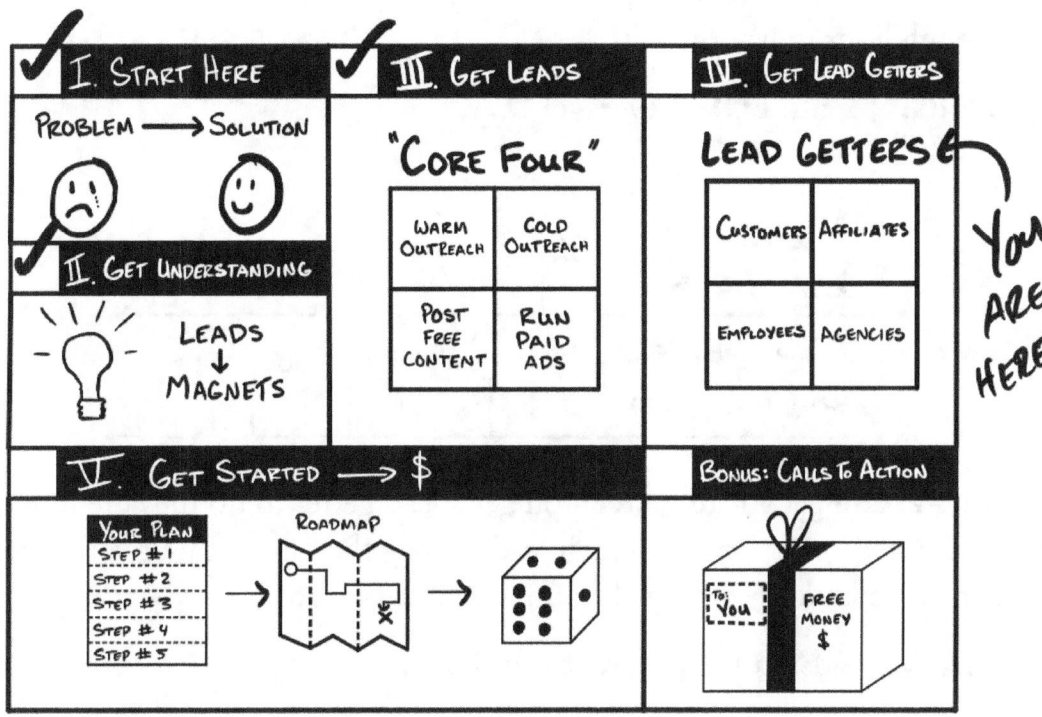

Lead Getters Give You Leverage

Alex Hormozi ✓
@AlexHormozi   ...

Only two people can let strangers know about the stuff you sell:
1) You
2) Other people

There are more of them than you.

People can find out about the stuff we sell from two sources. *We* can let them know using the core four. Or, *other people* can let them know using the core four. I call these other people

lead getters. When other people do it for us, we save time. That means we get more engaged leads for less work. Leverage baby.

Imagine four scenarios:

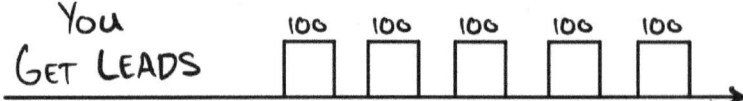

Scenario #1: You <u>are</u> the lead getter. You do the core four all day everyday by yourself. You get enough leads to pay the bills.

Work: HIGH Leads: LOW Leverage: LOW

Scenario #2: You <u>get</u> a lead getter. You get a lead getter to do the core four on your behalf. Now, the lead getter brings enough leads to pay the bills without you advertising. You work less than scenario #1 and get the same number of leads.

Work: LOW. Leads: LOW. Leverage: HIGH.

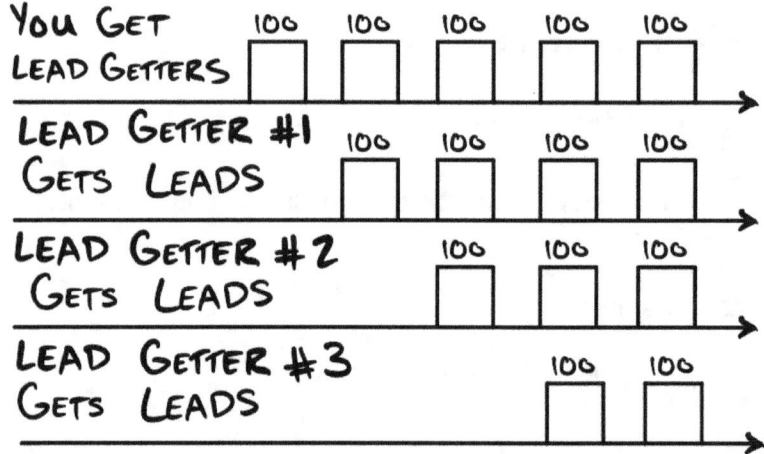

Scenario #3: You get lots of lead getters. You spend all your time getting other lead getters. Your leads go up every time you get another one. You work all day everyday, but you get way more leads than you did when it was just you. You work more than scenario #2 but get *way* more leads.

Work: HIGH. Leads: HIGH. Leverage: HIGHER.

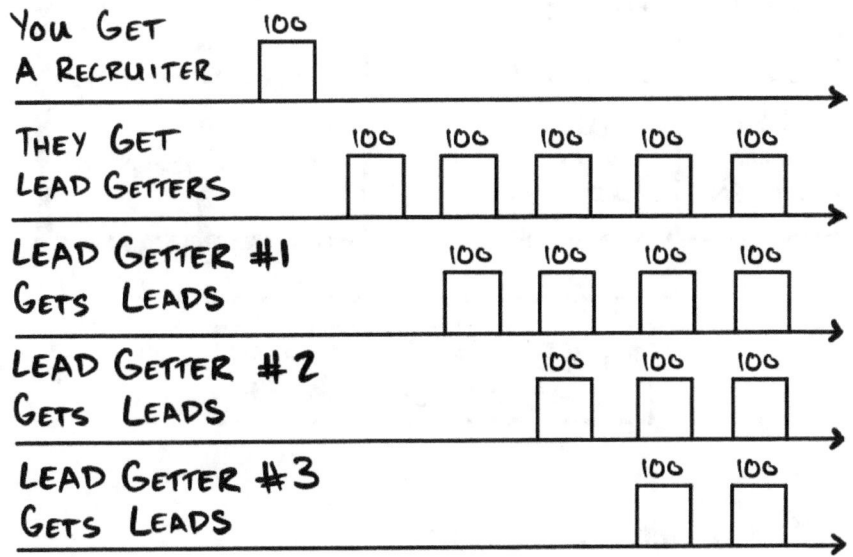

Scenario #4: You get a lead getter who gets lead getters. You recruit somebody who recruits other people to advertise on your behalf. They get more lead getters every month. You only had to work to get the first lead getter *once*, but his leads continue climbing without you working. You work less than scenario #3, and you get more leads each and every month.

Work: LOW. Leads: HIGH. Leverage: HIGHEST.

Now you've got the makings of a *$100M Leads* machine.

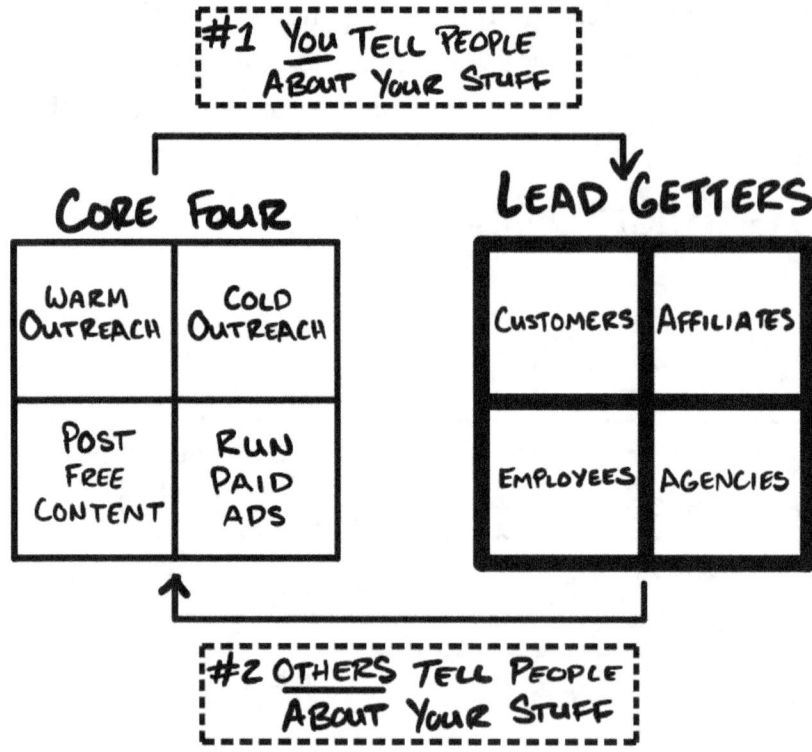

Outline of The "Lead Getters" Section

The lead getters aren't part of the "core four" because they're not things you do. But you have to do the core four to get them. Once you get them, they do it for you. The process repeats - lead getters can go get lead getters!

Lead getters start out as leads, then become engaged leads. The difference is they get other people interested in your stuff too. Ideally, every lead becomes a lead getter.

The four lead getters are:

#1 Customers- they buy your stuff then tell other people about it to get you leads.

#2 Employees- people in your business that get you leads.

#3 Agencies- businesses with services that get you leads.

#4 Affiliates- businesses who tell their audiences about your stuff to get you leads.

All four let other people know about your stuff, providing higher leverage than doing it on your own. Understanding these four lead getters allows you to build a lead getting machine for every company you start.

This section will break down how to use all four, their differences, how to work with them, when to use them, best practices, and how to measure progress.

FREE GIFT: Advanced Bonus - Get People To Do It For You

That may have been one of my favorite chapters in the book. It took me so so long to figure out how to recombine everything into a simple model. If you want even more training on getting other people to get you leads, and how it applies to scaling go to: Acquisition.com/training/leads. And as always, you can also scan the QR code below if you hate typing.

#1 Customer Referrals - Word of Mouth

"The best source of new work, is the work on your desk" — Charlie Munger

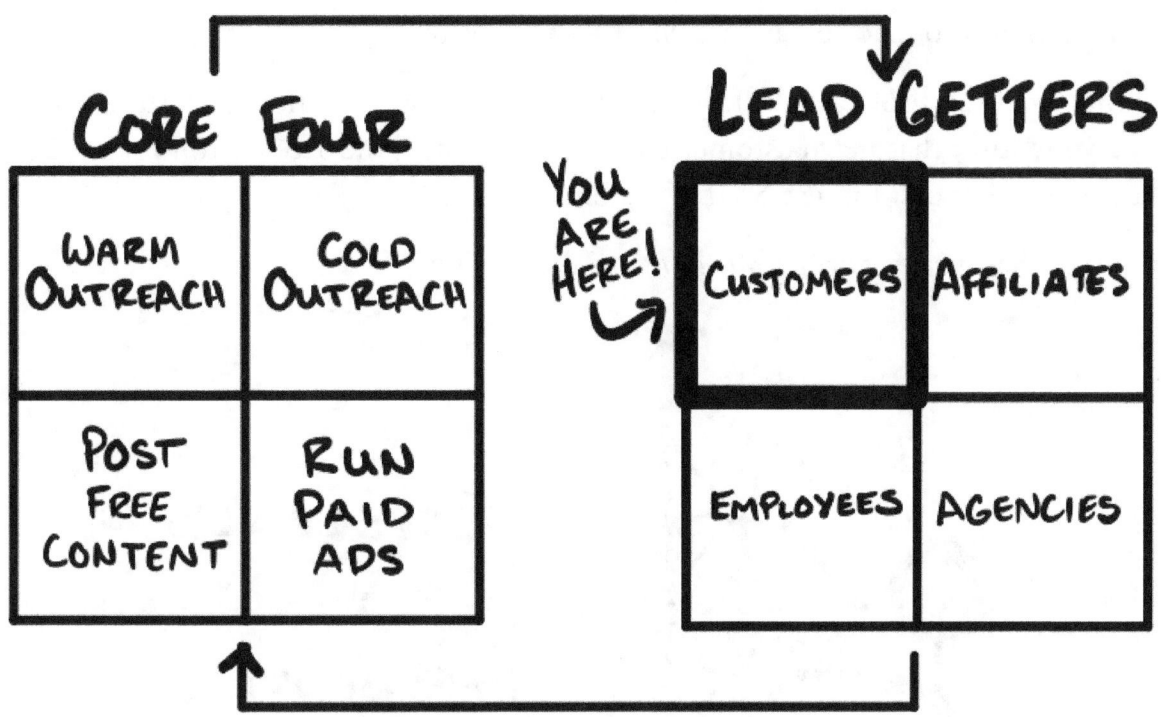

How Referrals Work

A referral happens when somebody, a referrer, sends an engaged lead to your business. Anyone can refer, but the best referrals come from your customers. So this chapter focuses on getting more referrals from your customers.

How Referrals Grow Your Business

Referrals are important because they grow your business in two ways:

1. **They're worth more (higher LTGP).** Referrals buy more expensive stuff and buy it more times. They also tend to pay in cash upfront. Lovely.

2. **They cost less (lower CAC).** If one customer sends you another customer because they like your stuff, that new customer costs you nothing. And free customers are cheaper than customers that cost money. So free customers = good.

On top of that, *referrals are exponential.* Let me explain.

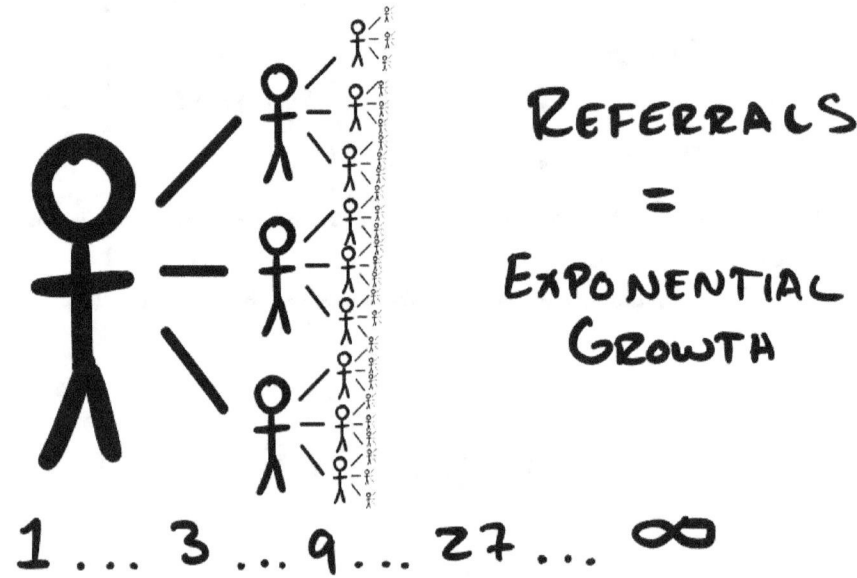

The number of engaged leads you get from the core four depends on how much you do them. It's a pretty linear relationship. But with word of mouth, we can do even better - it's exponential. One customer brings two, two bring four, four bring eight, and so forth. Nothing scales like word of mouth. You can quantify it using the referral growth equation: Referrals (in) minus churned customers (out).

- If referrals are greater than churn: you grow without any other advertising (yay!)

- If referrals are equal to churn: you need other advertising to grow your business (meh)

- If referrals are less than churn: you've got to advertise to break even (boo - most folks)

With referrals, you can maintain growth *no matter how big you get*. On the other hand, small businesses barely scrape by because they have about the same customers exiting as they do entering. A hamster wheel of death. Here's why…

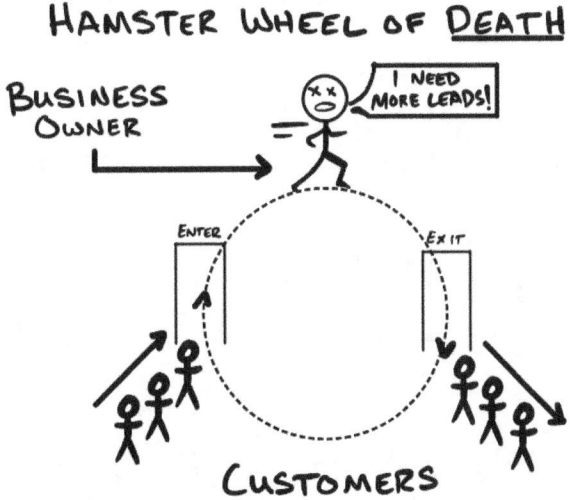

Two Reasons Most Businesses Don't Get Referrals

Most businesses don't get referrals for two reasons. First, their product isn't as good as they think it is. Second, they don't ask for them.

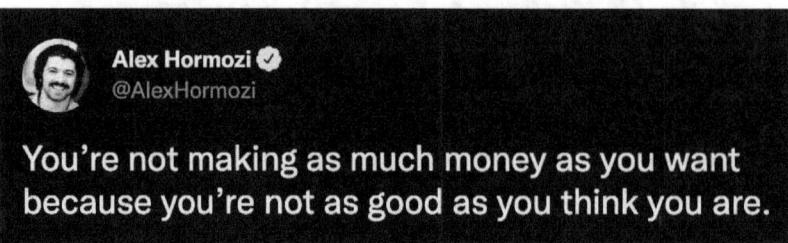

<u>Problem #1: The Product Isn't Good Enough</u>

If your product were exceptional, people would already know about it and you'd have more business than you could handle. So if you sell direct to consumers and they are not bringing you more customers, your product has room to improve. I like to ask myself: "Why are my customers too embarrassed to tell everyone they know about my product?" Most of the stuff I pay for, kind of sucks. Business owners wonder why they don't get referrals. The answer is right in front of them. They're just not good enough.

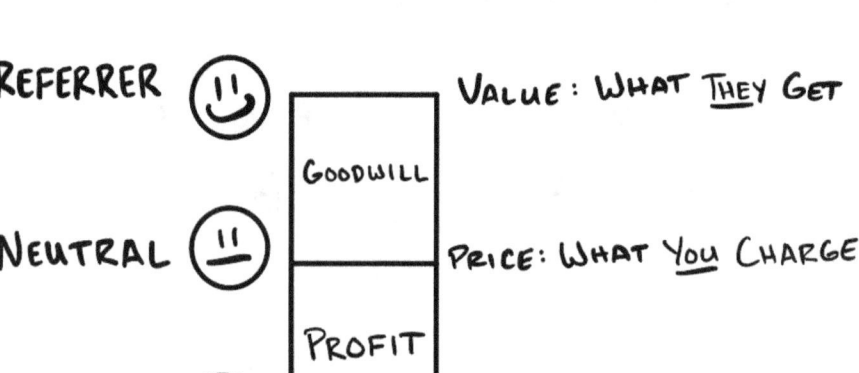

Price is what you charge. Value is what they get. *The difference between price and value is* **goodwill**. There are two ways to build goodwill with your customers: you can lower your price or you can give more value. To build goodwill to get referrals, the question isn't how do we lower our price but, how do we give more value?

Six Ways To Get More Referrals By <u>Giving</u> More Value

There are six ways I get referrals by giving more value. And it just so happens to map to the parts of an ad. Neat-o.

1) Call Outs → Sell Better Customers

2) Dream Outcome → Set Better Expectations

3) Increase Perceived Likelihood of Achievement → Get More People Better Results

4) Decrease Time Delay → Get Faster Results

5) Decrease Effort and Sacrifice → Keep Making Your Stuff Better

6) Call to Action → Tell Them What To Buy Next

1. Call outs → Sell Better Customers. We want to sell better customers because they get the most value from our products. Customers that get the most value have the most good will and refer the most.

> **Exercise #37: Increase the quality of the prospect, and you'll increase the quality of the product.** Figure out what your most successful customers have in common. Use those similarities to target a new audience that has the greatest chance of getting the most value. Then, sell <u>only</u> people who meet those new criteria. Set yourself up to build more goodwill. More goodwill means more referrals.

SET BETTER EXPECTATIONS

UNDERPROMISE OVERDELIVER > OVERPROMISE UNDERDELIVER

2. Dream Outcome → Set Better Expectations: The fastest, easiest, and cheapest way to make your product remarkable - make it better than they expect. And that's easier than you might think because *you* set the expectations.

Exercise #38: *Slowly* **lower the promises you make when making offers.** Keep lowering them until your close rates lower. At that point, stop. This maximizes how many customers you get *and* the goodwill you build with them. Maximized customers and goodwill means more referrals.

GET MORE PEOPLE BETTER RESULTS

90% SUCCESS RATE > 10% SUCCESS RATE

3. Increase Perceived Likelihood of Achievement → Get More People Better Results: Figure out what your best customers *do* to get the most value, and help other customers do the same. Track customer activities and compare average customers to the best ones.

Exercise #39: Improve your product.

1. Survey customers to find those with best results

2. Interview them to find out what they did differently

3. Look at the actions they had in common

4. Force new customers to repeat these actions

5. Measure improvement in average customer results

6. Match guarantee conditions to actions that get the best results

7. More success. More goodwill. More referrals.

4. Decrease Time Delay → Make Faster Wins: I define a "win" as any positive experience a customer has. Faster wins increase perception of speed, likelihood they'll stick, and how much they trust you. To make wins feel faster, give them wins more often.

Exercise #40: Make faster wins.

1. Deliver small things at shorter intervals rather than all at once

2. Share progress updates as frequently as possible

3. Force as many wins as possible in the first forty-eight hours after purchase

4. Always let customers know when they'll hear from you next.

5. Never expect customers to forgive you - add fifty percent to timelines to deliver early.

ON-GOING VALUE

$.....$.....$.....$.....$.....

5. Decrease Effort & Sacrifice → Keep Making Your Stuff Better: If customers do less stuff they hate or give up fewer things they love to benefit from your product, you've made it better. There's no such thing as a perfect product - you can always make it better. The easier you make it for them to benefit, the more goodwill you get, and the more likely they'll refer.

Exercise #41: Keep improving your stuff.

1. Find the most common problem using customer service data, surveys, and reviews

2. Figure out your fix, getting feedback from successful customers

3. Improve your product based on feedback

4. Test new version with small group of struggling customers

5. Get next round of feedback; roll out if problem solved, or return to Step 2

6. Move to next most common problem and repeat

6. Call To Action → Tell Them What To Buy Next: If you have an amazing product, customers will want more. You have to satisfy their desire to buy, or they'll buy *from someone else*. Sell them again - either a new thing or more of what they just bought. This gets you more goodwill and extends customer lifetime.

> **Exercise #42: Treat every customer like it's the first time you've sold them.** Make your next offer more compelling than your first. Remind them to buy more after each big win. More things to buy means more opportunities to add value. More value means more goodwill. And more goodwill means more referrals.

One Question to Rule Them All

Let's consolidate these six steps into one thought experiment. I encourage you to try it out with your team. Here it is: *You've lost all your customers but one. The gods of advertising ban you from doing the core four and decree: 1) All customers must come from this one customer. 2) Violate our terms and we will destroy your business.*

How would you treat this customer? What would you do to make their experience so valuable they would send all their friends? What kind of results would they need to get? What would their onboarding be? What type of customer would you pick?

> **Exercise #43:** Think about it. Write it out. *Your business depends on it. Then... do it :)*
>
> Type of customer?_____
>
> Results? _____
>
> Onboarding? _____
>
> On-going experience? _____
>
> _____

Referrals: Ask For Them

Do you know why businesses have so few referrals compared to what they could have? They never ask for them.

Seven Ways To Ask For Referrals

There are three components to a referral program: how you give the incentive, what you incentivize with, and how you ask. Here are the seven combos that worked best for me:

1. One-Sided Referral Benefit: Pay your average CAC to the referrer or the friend.

2. Two-Sided Referral Benefits: Pay CAC to both parties, split between referrer and friend.

3. Ask For A Referral Right When They Buy: Get names and numbers of potential referrals at point of sale.

4. Add Referrals As A Negotiation Chip: Offer discounts in exchange for introductions to friends.

5. Referral Events: Run time-limited promotions where people get rewards for bringing friends.

6. Ongoing Referral Programs: Consistently promote the benefits of doing things with others.

7. Unlockable Referral Bonuses: Create bonuses for people who refer and leave testimonials.

The more insane you make the offer, the more people will refer. If you want them to refer, make it so good they'd be stupid not to.

> **Exercise #44: Pick a referral strategy. Let your customers know about it.**

Combine Referral Strategies To Get More Referrals

Example combination.

Give everyone a gift card for one-third the cost of their program. Tell them they can give it to a friend of theirs if they sign up with them. Give the gift card an expiration date within seven to fourteen days from the date you give it to them→it'll force them to use it. This gives the referrer status when they give it to their friend. Rather than saying "Hey join my program for $2000 off" they say, "I got this gift card for $2000. Do you want it? I don't want to waste it." It's seen as a much bigger deal for them and you.

You can still use the three-way introduction with this tactic. Then text a picture of the gift card. Bonus points if you write the friend's name on it before texting the picture. It makes it feel personalized and gives you a legitimate reason for asking for their friend's name (wink).

PS - You can also sell the gift cards at ninety percent off as purchasable gifts (only for friends of customers). The referrer looks like they spent a lot of money, and you get paid to get new customers. I can hardly think of a better way to make money. Again, the only limit is your creativity.

> **Exercise #45: Do it.** Figure out your referral percentages and churn percentages to set a baseline. Implement the six "giving value" steps to build goodwill. Then capitalize on that goodwill, using one or more of the seven ways to ask for referrals.

Next Up...

To scale our ads, we need help. You're gonna need it if you wanna make the *big money*. Next up, employees...

FREE GIFT: BONUS - Customer Referral Frenzy

If you want to know more about ways to use the highest leverage, most profitable way of getting customers, I made a training just for you. You can get it here for free: Acquisition.com/training/leads. And as always, you can also scan the QR code below if you hate typing.

#2 Employees

"If you want to go fast, go alone. If you want to go far, go together" — *African Proverb*

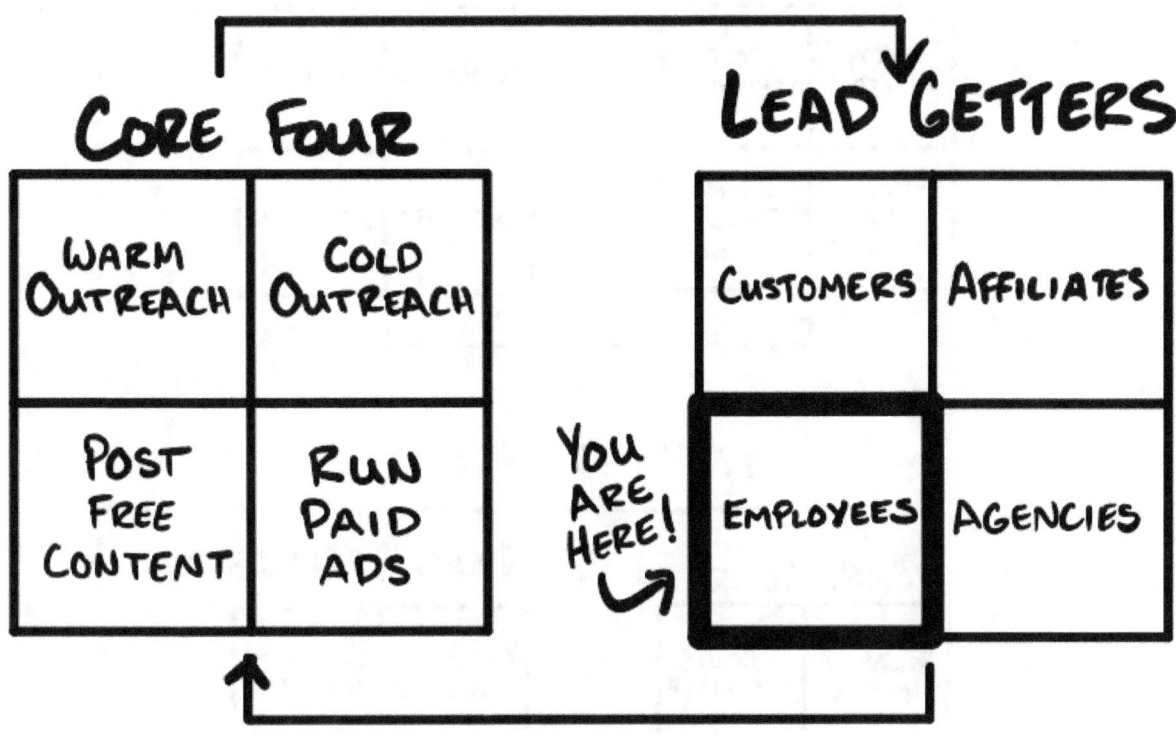

How Employees Work To Get You Leads

Lead-getting employees are people working in your business that you train to get you leads. They can run ads, make and post content, and do outreach - any advertising you train them to do. More lead-getting employees means more engaged leads for your business and less work you have to do.

<u>Bottom Line</u>: Employees make a fully functioning enterprise that grows without you.

How To Get Employee Leads: The Internal Core Four

Remember the core four? Well, they work for getting employees too. By changing the frame from "letting potential customers know about your stuff" to "letting potential employees know about your stuff" it immediately turns into something you already know how to do. Employees are just other people you let know about your stuff. So you do the same thing!

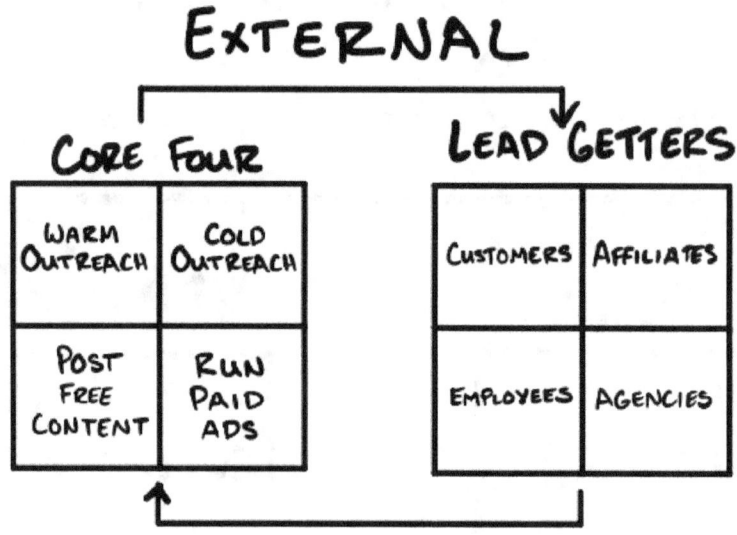

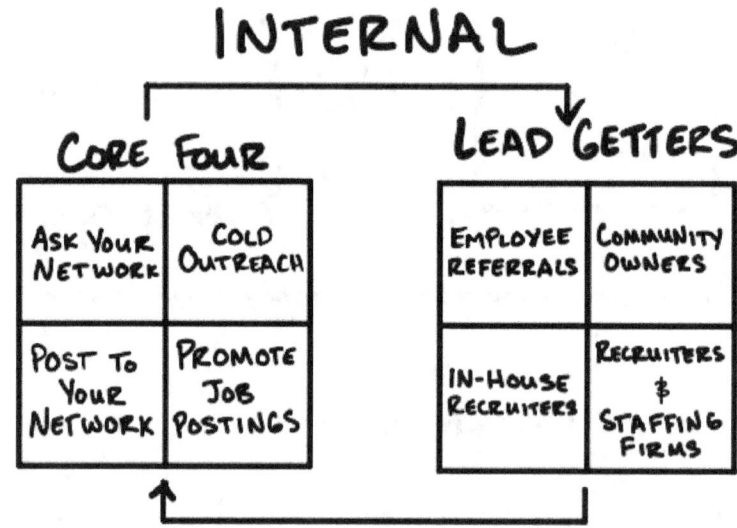

Line up the actions to get employees with the actions to get customers. It's the same stuff!

Customers → Employees

Warm Outreach→Asking Your Network

Cold Outreach→ Recruiting

Post Content→Posting Job Openings

Paid Ads→Promoting Job Postings

Customer Referrals→Employee Referrals

Affiliates→ Associations, Guilds, Listservs etc.

Agencies→ Staffing firms etc.

Employees→Employees (unchanged)

The ways you get employee leads and their lead getters have equivalents to the ways you get customer leads and *their* lead getters. And like creating a reliable process to get customers, you can also create a reliable process of getting employees. You'll need <u>both</u> to scale.

How To Get Employees To Get You Leads

Now you hire someone who costs you money every month. Let's make sure you make it back, and some ASAP. If you can't afford people who already know how to get leads, your next best option is to train them. Approach training with this 3Ds mental model: Document, Demonstrate, Duplicate.

Step One - Document: *Make a checklist.* Write down the steps exactly as you do it. Record yourself doing the thing multiple ways and in multiple shifts. Can you do an A+ job only following your directions exactly? If so, you have the first draft of your checklist.

> **Exercise #46: Make your checklist.** Follow your own instructions. See if it works. Adjust until you get the result *only* following the checklist you made.

Step Two - Demonstrate: *Do it in front of them.* Walk them through the checklist step by step. Adjust your checklist if they stop you or slow you down to understand something.

Step Three - Duplicate: *They do it in front of you.* Have them follow the same checklist you followed. Fix your checklist until it's right. Then, have them follow it until they get it right.

After training your first few employees, you'll have worked out the kinks for that job. If you vanished tomorrow, could a stranger get the results you get if they only followed your checklist? That's the level of clarity to shoot for. Some helpful notes on training:

- If they get it wrong or get confused, we got it wrong or made it confusing.

- If they only "get it" after long explanations, we've got work to do.

- There's a difference between competence and performance. Sometimes they just need practice.

- Focus on their ability to follow directions more than the result.

- Let them know when they do a step successfully.

- If they follow directions exactly and get the wrong result, praise them and correct the checklist.

- Avoid punishment during training. Reward good stuff you want them to do more of.

- Give feedback one step at a time.

- Retrain the team whenever there's a major dip from normal performance.

- Once training works on new trainees, I shorten my window for judging performance.

How to Calculate Returns From Lead-Getting Employees

Excluding paid ads, the cost of advertising with employees is almost entirely based on payroll. We compare how much we spend on payroll to how much money the engaged leads bring in. Calculate cost per engaged lead, then multiply by the number of engaged leads it takes to get a customer to get CAC. Compare CAC to LTGP to get your LTGP : CAC ratio.

How To Know Which Employees to Focus On To Maximize Returns

If your cost to get a customer is within 3x industry average then you're doing *good enough*. From there, you focus on bumping up your LTGP. If your CAC is more than 3x industry average then you have a sales problem or an advertising problem. Diagnose with this question: *Do my engaged leads have the problem I solve and the money to spend?*

- If no, then they're not qualified–that's an advertising problem.
- If yes, then they're qualified and:
    o They're buying but you don't have enough of them–advertising problem
    o They're qualified but not buying–sales problem.

Make sure you retrain or rehire people closest to the actual problem.

The Next Lead Getter…

The next stop on our advertising journey leads us to agencies. I use them to shortcut my path to learning *anything*.

FREE GIFT: BONUS TUTORIAL - Build or Buy - The Talent Roadmap

The longer I do business, the more I ask "who" over what and how. This training may be one of the most tactical and important, because no matter what you want to build, you're gonna need help. Since it's so important, I made a training outlining this content in more depth with some downloads etc. You can watch it free at Acquisition.com/training/leads. As always, you can also scan the QR code below if you hate typing.

#3 Agencies

"Everything is for sale"

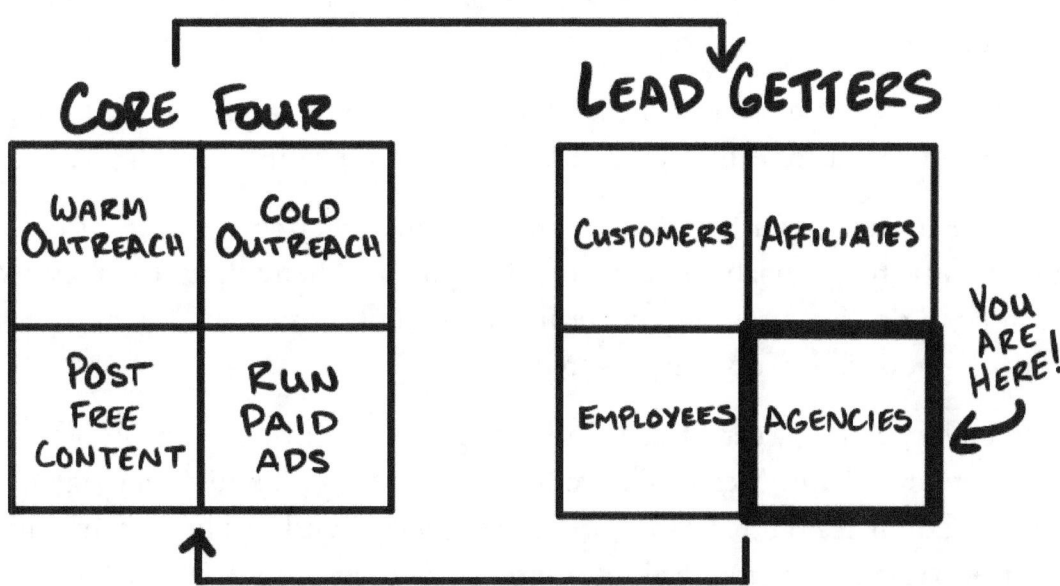

Good agencies cost money, so if you have no money, they're out of the question. But if you do have some money, use agencies for learning new methods and new platforms. I hire agencies offering new ways to do content, outreach, or paid ads because they've already made the big mistakes. I also use agencies when I want to start advertising on a platform I don't understand. Hiring an agency is all about investing in important skills you can't really learn anywhere else, without losing time and attention you could have used to learn other important stuff that scales your business. This chapter breaks hiring an agency down into two steps:

1. How I use agencies now. And how you can, too.

2. How to pick the right agency

How I Use Agencies Now. And How You Can Too.

Here's how I use agencies now. Rather than believe the lie that "I'll never have to learn this stuff because they can do it," I start every agency relationship with a purpose and a deadline to fulfill it. I open by saying:

"I want to do what you do in my business, but I don't know how. I'd like to work with you for 6 months so I can learn how you do it. Plus, I'll pay extra for you to break down why you make the decisions you do and the steps you take to make them. Then, after I get a good idea of how it all works, I'll start training my team on it. And once they can do it well enough, I'd like to change to a lower cost consulting arrangement. This way, you can still help us if we run into problems. Are you opposed to this?"

In my experience, most agencies are not opposed to teaching you their methods. Be willing to negotiate - at some price, it's worth it for both of you.

If you're upfront about your intentions and the agency agrees, you get better short-term results because they probably know more than you, and better long-term results because you learn how to do it yourself or your team learns to do it for you. You also spend the maximum amount of time with their best reps.

Remember, you only get a fraction of the agency's attention, so results get worse whenever they get new clients. Meanwhile, your team gets better because they stay focused on you full-time. Compare your team's results to the agency's until you beat them. Then, cancel the relationship and put the money into scaling everything you just learned.

Exercise #47: Use the script above as your guide to set terms with them and deadlines when you begin talking to agencies. Be OK with negotiating a bit to make it work.

How to Pick The Right Agency

After working with tons of bad agencies, and a handful of good ones, I created a list of what all the good ones had in common:

1. Someone you know got good results with them.

2. Prominent companies got good results working with them.

3. They have a waiting list.

4. They have a clear sales process that sets realistic expectations.

5. They focus on long-term strategy, not short-term hacks.

6. They tell you exactly what they need from you and how they'll use it.

7. They suggest regular meetings and offer several ways to update you on progress.

8. They give updates in simple terms and have clear ways to track costs against results.

9. They make a good offer:

   - Dream outcome aligns with what you want
   - Show how many similar clients they've helped
   - Provide clear timelines
   - Explain what effort and sacrifice they require from you

10. They are expensive. All good agencies are expensive… but not all expensive agencies are good.

Exercise #48: Pick your agency. Once an agency checks these boxes, they're worth considering. Talk with a few more before you make a decision, even if they agree to your terms upfront. Compare them using the checklist above, and then pick the best one for you.

Conclusion

Even though this isn't the "traditional" agency model, *both* businesses benefit. They get a customer they otherwise wouldn't have. And we get a money-making skill for life. Win-win.

Next Steps:

1) Decide if using an agency makes sense for you right now.

2) Talk to a lot of agencies to get a feel for the market. Don't be cheap.

3) Use the agreement framework I outlined.

4) Set a clear deadline to force you (and your team) to learn the skills.

5) Use both teams until yours beats theirs regularly.

6) Switch to discounted consulting until you feel like you're teaching them instead of them teaching you…then cut 'em loose.

Now that we know how to profit from the high risk world of agencies, we explore the lead-getter that's made me the most money. We recruit an army of businesses who can get us even more leads - *affiliates*.

FREE GIFT: What To Look For in An Agency Checklist

If you want to know the best way to use agencies, rather than being used by them, I made a free training for you. You can watch it free at: Acquisition.com/training/leads. It has swipe files and some other goodies. As always, you can also scan the QR code below if you hate typing.

#4 Affiliates and Partners

"Nothing makes friends like money"

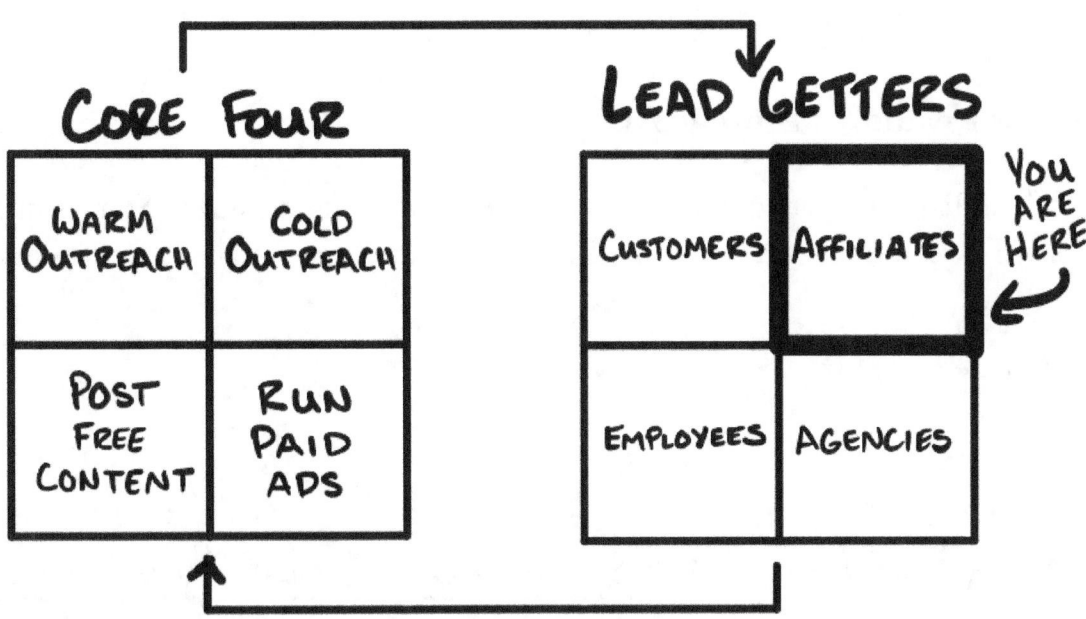

How Affiliates Work

An **affiliate** is a lead-getter. They are an independent business that tells their audience to buy *your* stuff. Affiliates seem like referrals on the outside, but are much different under the hood. First, they have their own businesses and do their own advertising. Second, they agree to offer *your* stuff to *their* engaged leads in exchange for money, free stuff, or both.

Now, you get affiliates by advertising and then making them offers *just like you would customers.* But, affiliates demand a unique type of offer. Instead of offering your product, you offer a fast, simple, and easy way to make commissions promoting it. And that can mean literally millions of engaged leads to your business. So this makes affiliates one of the highest-leverage lead-getters out there.

Why You Want An Affiliate Army

Each affiliate you get adds another *stream* of leads and customers. So recruiting, activating, then integrating with an army of affiliates causes crazy scaling, fast. That's good. We want that.

Compare these two scenarios:

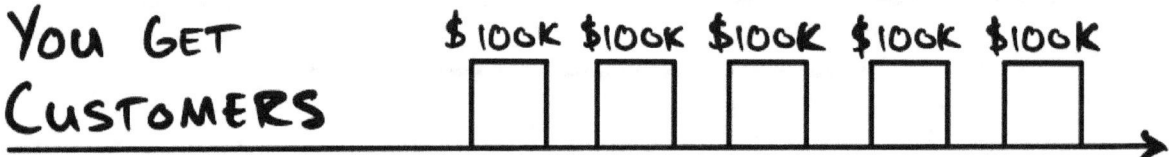

Scenario #1: You sell ten *customers* per month worth $10,000 each. Your business caps at $100,000 per month. In twelve months you've made 1.2 million. Assuming no other advertising, your business *plateaus*. Low-Leverage.

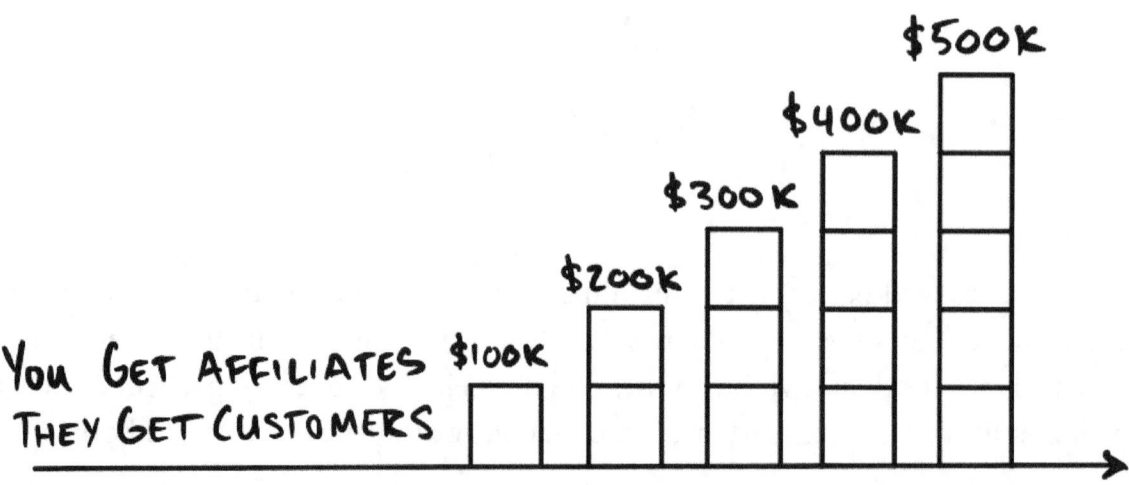

Scenario #2: For the same effort, you sell ten *affiliates* per month. Each month, those affiliates bring you *one* of those $10,000 customers. Now, every single month you add an *extra* $100,000 in revenue. In twelve months you've made *7.8 million*. And it grows *every month thereafter*. Same work, more money. High-Leverage.

How To Build An Affiliate Army in Six Steps

Step 1: Find Your Ideal Affiliates

Step 2: Make Them an Offer

Step 3: Qualify Them

Step 4: Figure Out What To Pay Them

Step 5: Get Them Advertising

Step 6: Keep Them Advertising

That's it. Let's dive in.

Step 1: Find Your Ideal Affiliate

The ideal affiliate has a business with a warm audience full of people like your customers. Start making a list of those businesses. If none come to mind, answer these questions about your best customers:

What do they buy? → *Who provides that stuff?*

Where do they go? → *What businesses are in those surrounding areas?*

What do they like to do? → *Who provides those services?*

If direct to consumer—the employers of your consumers could make great affiliates:

What types of businesses do they work for? What kinds of jobs do they have?

In a nutshell… *Who's got my leads!?*

Exercise #49: Make a sheet with each of these questions and categories. This list should take up a few pages. Search online to fill it in. If you struggle, call up your customers and ask them! <u>End result</u>: Create a lead list of your highest potential affiliates.

Step 2: Make Them An Offer

We make the affiliate-offer and advertise it the same way we would any other offer, calling out our audience, showing our value elements, and then calling them to action. Since affiliates are businesses, or start a business by signing up, you offer them a new way to make money.

<u>Call out:</u>

Call outs for potential affiliates often include:

- The affiliate business owners themselves - *ATTENTION SPA OWNERS*

- The affiliate's customers - *Do you work with busy professionals who spend all day in meetings?*

- Results the affiliate businesses promise - *To the heroes who heal the stress of others…*

- Products and services the affiliates deliver - *If you sell lotions or scented oils this is for you…*

- To our own customers - *Do you know anyone who owns a spa?*

Now that we can grab a potential affiliate's attention - let's make it worth their while…

Exercise #50: Pick your call out and fill in the blanks below to complete your offer.

Make more money from your current customers and get more leads than your current offer (dream outcome)

_____

…with a high chance of working since your customers already want the product (perceived likelihood of achievement)

_____

...without needing to build, deliver, or provide customer support for the product yourself (effort and sacrifice)

_____

...so you can start selling it tomorrow (time delay).

_____

_____

Step 3: Qualify Them

Potential affiliates become actual affiliates when they understand and agree to your terms. We want to get them their first win as fast as possible, so we set up our terms to force them to win quickly. I do that by getting them to invest their time, money, and in the product itself. Here are two ways I get affiliates invested and winning:

Way #1: Make Them A Customer: Make them buy and preferably use the product to keep affiliate status. The more money an affiliate invests in your product, the more money they make.

Way #2: Make Them An Expert: Make them pay for onboarding and training that certifies them as a product expert. This covers some advertising costs and means I can afford proper onboarding and training for every affiliate.

How much to charge? I recommend 10-20% of what the average <u>active</u> affiliate makes in the first twelve months. It's enough to get them invested but not so much to scare them off.

Bottom Line: Make your affiliates customers, experts, or both (my favorite way). If you don't get enough people to start, lower the commitment. If you don't get enough people to follow through, raise it.

Step 4: Figure Out What To Pay Them

The first biggest problem to solve with affiliates is getting them bought in. The second biggest problem with affiliates is *keeping them bought in*, which depends on how you reward them. When figuring out ways to pay affiliates, I look at two basic things: what they get paid for and how much they get paid.

1. What They Get Paid For: I pay affiliates for new customers and repeat customers. You can also pay them for steps before someone becomes a customer, like lead magnets downloaded or appointments set.

2. How Much They Get Paid: I suggest paying affiliates based on your maximum allowable cost to acquire a customer (CAC). I recommend a three-tier payout structure:

- Tier 1: 25% of CAC for anyone who agrees to initial terms
- Tier 2: 50% of CAC once they activate
- Tier 3: 100% of CAC once they sustain a level of performance

This tiered method has a hidden profitable side effect: the average payout is much less than your maximum allowable CAC, leaving "leftover" profit for contests, advertising, or incentivizing rising stars.

Exercise #51: Figure out what you want to pay your affiliates.

What they get paid for: _____

How much they get paid in Tier 1: _____

How much they get paid in Tier 2: _____

How much they get paid in Tier 3: _____

How often they get paid (weekly, bi-weekly, monthly) _____

_____

Step 5: Get Them Advertising - Launch

Like referrers, how much value affiliates get from you determines how much they advertise your stuff. So, treat them like customers. Give them something good, fast. Nothing does that for affiliates like big launches and lots of cash.

Launches work by having affiliates advertise your lead magnet or core offer to their audience before they can buy it. I use the whisper-tease-shout method for launches (of any kind, not just affiliates):

Whisper: *Think "Call Outs."* Like an ad, the key to the whisper phase is *curiosity*. Keep the product itself mysterious and hint at how big of a deal it is. Start whispering every four to six weeks until you get sixty days out. Then whisper every two to three weeks until you get thirty days out. Then, start teasing…

Tease: *Think "Elements Of Value."* It's time to start satisfying all the curiosity you created during the whisper phase. Reveal your product, make the date of the launch public, and start _showing_ the elements of value. Use the What-Who-When Framework from the paid ads chapter. Start teasing once per week until fourteen days out. Then tease twice per week until three days out. Three days out, it's time to shout from the rooftops.

Shout: *Think "Call to Action."* Give specific actions for the audience to take when the product launches. Now you start pounding the audience with bonuses, scarcity, urgency, and guarantees around being "the first ones." You shout to get as many people exposed to your offer as you can. Shout at least twice a day starting three days out. On the day of, start shouting every few hours until two hours out. Then shout every thirty minutes until you launch the product.

Bottom Line: Get your affiliates to launch. Set them up with everything they need to do the whisper-tease-shout right. They do the advertising. You get the engaged leads. *Everyone* gets paid.

Step 6: Keep Them Advertising

The strategy we use to start them advertising differs from the one we use to keep them advertising. In an ideal world, you sell an affiliate once and they send engaged leads for life. Integration gets us there.

I've got three ways you can integrate your product into their offer. First, you can get them to _give away your lead magnet_ with every purchase of their stuff. Second, you can get them to _sell your lead magnet separately_ to their audience. Third, you can get them to directly _sell your core offer_. I ordered from easiest to hardest:

1. Affiliates Give Your Lead Magnet Away When Somebody Buys Their Stuff: The idea here is for your lead magnet to make the affiliate's offer more valuable, allowing them to charge more for it and get more leads than they could without it. The best lead magnets give away a free trial or sample of your thing, reveal a problem, or offer a single step of a multi-step solution. For example, if I sell massages, I recruit the personal training studio next door as an affiliate. Everyone who buys personal training from them gets a free massage from me, making their offer stronger and getting us more leads.

2. Affiliates Sell Your Lead Magnet: Basically, the affiliate can sell anything of yours that turns their customers into your customers. It could be a book, an event, a service, software, a sample product, etc. Giving affiliates all the cash from selling a lead magnet you fulfill becomes all profit and no work for them. Your money comes by selling your main thing for more than it cost you to deliver your lead magnet. For example, the gyms would sell a nutrition consult with us and keep the money, and we'd upsell our products during the consult.

3. Affiliates Sell Your Core Offer: An affiliate sells your core offer directly to their customers and adds another source of income without extra work. For some affiliates, this is their entire source of income. Many companies offer this structure as either a new business opportunity or a bolt-on to the affiliate's existing business. When you do it this way, the affiliate will get a higher percentage of your lifetime gross profit. For example, they sell your entire massage package or your entire program or services, and you split the money.

After testing, we continue to do Strategy 1 (twice per year as a big event) and Strategy 3 on an ongoing basis. Many similar businesses in our portfolio use Strategy 2. Integration is the long-term strategy for using affiliates to get enduring lead flow. Treat affiliates like customers. Make your offer make sense for their business and make it so good they'd feel stupid saying no.

> **Exercise #52: Fully integrate with your affiliate. Pick whether you want them to:**
>
> ☐ Give your lead magnet away.
> ☐ Sell your lead magnet.
> ☐ Sell your core offer directly.

Costs and Returns

When calculating returns with other methods, we compare lifetime gross profit (LTGP) with the cost to acquire a customer (CAC). With affiliates, we spend money to get affiliates, and the return comes from the customers they bring us. To calculate returns, we compare the cost of acquiring an affiliate with the gross profit from all the customers they bring.

We aim for a ratio of at least 3:1, and to improve it, we can lower CAC, increase LTGP, or both. Affiliates are partners who promote your products for mutual benefit, so treat them like customers and deliver more value than their costs.

Conclusion

There are two ways to create a compounding business. You can find more people that never stop buying your stuff or you can find more people who never stop selling it for you. Referrals are the former. Affiliates are the ladder.

Advertise your affiliate offer until you get ten to twenty affiliates. Get results with those affiliates and use their feedback to work the kinks out of your offer, terms, launches, and integration strategy. Then, scale like crazy by turning their results into your first batch of affiliate lead magnets.

FREE GIFT: Build Your Affiliate Army BONUS

As you can see - I am a big fan of building affiliate programs when they're done right. To help you 'do it right' on your first try, I made an in depth video training for you. You can get it free at: Acquisition.com/training/leads. And as always, you can also scan the QR code below if you hate typing.

Section IV Conclusion: Get Lead Getters

*"The last skill you ever need to learn is how to get other
people to do everything you need for you."*

We do the core four to get engaged leads: warm outreach, post content, cold outreach, and paid ads. And we use them to get two types of engaged leads: the ones that become customers, or the ones we turn into lead getters. Lead getters come in four flavors: Referrers, Employees, Agencies, and Affiliates. Each have key strengths:

- Customer referrals have the biggest potential for low-cost exponential growth.

- Employees have your *direct* influence and run your business on your behalf.

- Agencies teach skills you keep forever and can transfer to your team.

- Affiliates, once you get them going, can operate entirely on their own.

You can either do the advertising or other people can. And there are more "other people" than there are of you. *You get more leads for the work you do when you have help.* So if you want to get a ton of leads, this is the way.

We covered a lot here. This section was how you scale: you get other people to help you. They are the missing link. Each has their own strategy and best practices. Use what applies to you now.

This leads us to Section V: Get Started. I want to put everything together for you in a nice bow so you know *exactly what to do next*. Together, we'll eliminate leads as the bottleneck in your business forever. Onwards!

SECTION V: GET STARTED

"It's not the end. It's not even the beginning of the end. But it is, perhaps, the end of the beginning"
— Winston Churchill

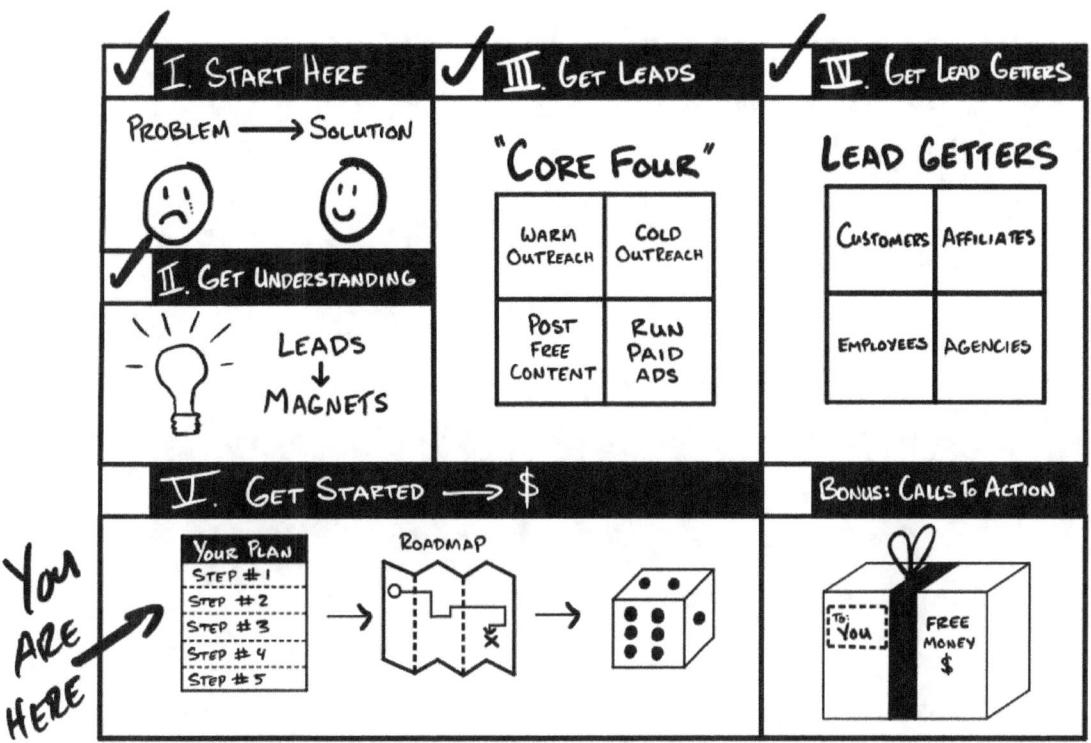

Outline Of The "Get Started" Section

This final section has three chapters. They are short and sweet, just like our time together.

In the first chapter, Advertising in real life– I'll lay out my one big advertising rule. Then, I'll give you my personal one-page advertising plan you can use to get more engaged leads, *today*.

In the next chapter, Putting It all Together– I'll lay out the roadmap to scale from your first few leads all the way to your *$100M Leads* machine.

Finally, A Decade In Page–I'll distill everything we learned into bullets to show how far we've come in our time together. Then, to send you on your way, I'll share a parable that has gotten me through even my hardest times.

Advertising in Real Life: Open To Goal

If some is good, more is better.

Rule of 100 on Steroids–Open To Goal

A successful gym chain allowed their sales managers to set their own schedules with the requirement of signing up five new members per day, no matter how long it took. I've found this "open-to-goal" approach common among elite entrepreneurs and salespeople. It focuses on outcomes rather than effort. It's similar to the rule of 100 but more advanced. You work until you achieve specific results, unlocking new levels of effort. To elevate your advertising, work until the job is done and focus on what is required, not just doing your best. Sometimes, your best needs to improve.

How I Make Open To Goal Work For Myself

If I had to pick the three habits that best served me in my life - they would be:

1) Waking up early (4-5 am)–Pro tip, this actually means *going to bed early…*

2) Getting right to work–No rituals. No routines. I drink coffee and get to work.

3) No meetings until noon–No interruptions. Nothing. Fully focused work time.

I don't believe there's any magic in waking up early, but there's magic in having a long stretch of uninterrupted work right after uninterrupted sleep. It's the most productive hours of my day, with nothing getting in my way. By setting a daily goal and focusing on dedicated work first, I've found waking up early and working straight for 8 hours to be my highest ROI habit. If you try it, I hope it serves you as well as it has served me. If the idea of working over twelve hours a day overwhelms you, start with fewer hours and build up. Some days it's tough, but I always like to remind myself:

"Do more than they do, and you will have more than they have."

Alex Hormozi ✔
@AlexHormozi

Whenever I get to a low point where I think "why do I even bother?"

I just try to remind myself "this is where most people stop, and this is why they don't win."

Since my job is usually to "get more customers" in most of my companies, advertising is what I focus on. This book, for example, was written exclusively in that open to goal time block.

So, if you're gonna follow my high ROI habit stack, then you're gonna want a clear action plan for that time. This is the simplest advertising plan I can give you.

One Page Advertising Checklist

Step #1: Pick The Type Of Engaged Lead To Get: Customers, Affiliates, Employees, or Agencies

Step #2: Pick Rule of 100 or Open To Goal. Commit To Your Daily Advertising Actions

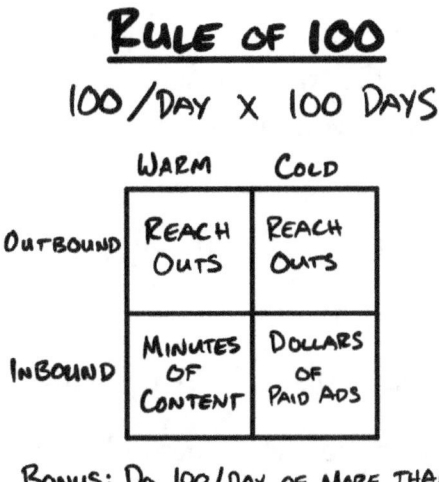

Step #3: Fill Out The Advertising Checklist For That Daily Action

Advertising Daily Checklist	
Who:	You
What:	Your Offer or Lead Magnet
Where:	Platform
To Whom:	Audience/List
When:	First 8 Hours
Why:	Get X Engaged Leads or Lead Getters
How:	Warm/ Cold Outreach, Content, Ads
How Much:	100 or Until you hit your goal
How Many:	# of Follow Ups/ Times Retargeted
How Long:	100 Days or Until you hit your goal

Step #4: Do this daily action until you have enough money to afford paying someone else to do it.

Step #5: When you do, go back to step 1. Make employees your new target lead type. And repeat steps 1-4 until you have the help you need. Then, scale again.

Conclusion

We're almost at the end. But, you don't have any more leads. What gives? Answer: Reading doesn't get people interested in the stuff you sell… *advertising does.* If you're not telling anyone about the stuff you sell, then you aren't getting anyone interested in the stuff you sell. Period.

This chapter laid out the plan to advertise in the simplest way I could:

- Work 'Open To Goal.'

- Structure your day to make Open To Goal possible.

- Create *and* commit to that goal with the one-page advertising checklist.

Harness the power of laying out your action steps on a *single page.* It leaves little room for excuses, distractions, and delusions. You either did the stuff or you didn't. You can fill out your one-page advertising checklist in about five minutes. And once the naked truth stares back at you, all you have left is to *do it.*

FREE GIFT: Downloadable Advertising Checklist

You can watch an added training and download this checklist to fill out for yourself at Acquisition.com/training/leads. As always, you can also scan the QR code below if you hate typing.

The Roadmap - Putting it All Together

Zero to $100,000,000

"A leader must aim high, see big, judge wisely, thus setting himself apart from the ordinary people who debate in narrow confines."
— *Charles de Gaulle, French President During World War II*

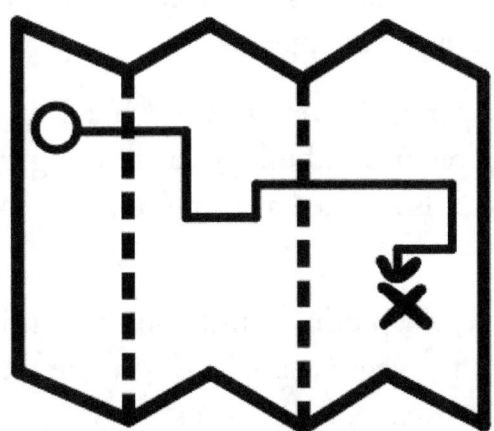

To get to where you want to go, it pays to know what lies ahead. So in this chapter, I describe the phases you will go through as you scale your advertising. Acquisition.com uses this roadmap to scale our portfolio companies from a few million a year, all the way to $100,000,000+. These levels will help you identify where you are on the advertising totem pole so you know what to do to get to the next level.

Level 1: *Your friends know about the stuff you sell.* To start getting engaged leads, you make one offer, to one avatar, on one platform. The moment you get engaged leads, is the moment you can start making money. For me, this started with reaching out to *everyone* I knew.

<u>Primary Action</u>: Warm outreach.

Level 2: *You <u>consistently</u> let <u>everyone you know</u> about the stuff you sell.* You know the exact inputs to get an engaged lead with your chosen advertising method. And, by scaling those inputs, you get *consistent* customers with it. But the consistent customers come from maximizing your personal work capacity. For me, on top of warm reach outs, I maximized my personal work capacity with paid aids, using a case study as my lead magnet. But looking back, I wish I would have started with posting free content. So I suggest that.

<u>Primary Actions</u>: Do as much warm outreach and post as much content as you can *consistently*.

Level 3: *You get employees to help you do more advertising.* You've maxed your personal advertising inputs, but not the platform. And if you want more engaged leads that can only mean one thing. Doing more. For me, I hired a videographer and a media buyer to take most of the paid ads work off my plate.

<u>Primary Action</u>: You hire people to advertise profitably on your behalf.

Level 4: *Your product is good enough to get consistent referrals.* You continue building goodwill and shoot for getting 25% or more of your customers from referrals. Now, you've set yourself up to ramp up your advertising again. But to make that work, you have to get more serious about hiring a team to make it happen.

This is when I realized that my ads were shut off but I was still getting referrals every week. So, I doubled down on referrals. I built goodwill using customer feedback to update my product every two weeks. I also started a strong referral program with big incentives at the same time.

<u>Primary Actions</u>: Focus on your product until you get consistent referrals then go back to scaling your advertising with a bigger team. This is where most people mess up. They let their product slip and never recover.

Level 5: *You advertise in more places in more ways with more people.* First, you expand to new audiences on your best platform. Then, you make ads with all placements and media types the platform supports. And, after your team can get consistent results, you expand your team again to add: *another platform, lead-getter, or core four activity.*

For me, I hit two birds with one stone. I expanded my paid ads to include potential affiliates. And this paved the way for my affiliate programs.

<u>Primary Action</u>: Advertise profitably using at least two methods on multiple platforms.

Level 6: *You hire killers.* Your executives grow departments specific to an advertising method or platform without you. And you're not looking for potential. You're looking for experienced leaders specializing in exactly what you want. We capped here.

It took me three years to figure out two things. One, that I needed veteran executives with experience suited to my problems. And two, that they needed stronger incentives. But by the time I realized this, I sold those companies. Once I started Acquisition.com I realized the power of expanding the pie to get more of the right people invested in winning. This is how we crossed $100M+ then $200M+ in portfolio revenue and beyond.

<u>Primary Action</u>: Get battle-hardened executives and department heads to take over new advertising activities and channels.

Level 7: I'll come back and edit this chapter once I cross a billion. I promise, I'll send the lessons as soon as I have them. You have my word.

Last Points: I know this looks clean. But it never is. Real business is *messy*. It takes *a lot* to find what audiences, lead magnets, methods, and platforms work best. And you can only find out what works if you try. So you have to try a lot of different things, a lot of different ways, for a long enough time to know for sure.

Nobody can ever know the absolute best thing to do. But I do know this: the more you advertise, the more people find out about the stuff you sell. The more people who know about the stuff you sell, the more people will buy it. This is the key to the *$100M Leads* Machine.

The $100M+ Lead Machine

Let's look into your future. Your business makes $100,000,000+ annual revenue. It's great to have a clear picture of what the $100M machine looks like. Let's have a look, shall we? First and foremost, your advertising fires on all cylinders…

• Your media team scales tons of free content, in all media types, on many platforms.

• You regularly make offers to your warm audience to get more customers or affiliates.

• Your ravenous audience makes *anything* you launch *immediately* profitable.

• You have teams running and scaling profitable paid ads across multiple platforms.

• Your cold outreach team gets you more customers.

• You have an affiliate manager launching and integrating all new affiliates.

• You have recruiters *and* recruiting agencies bringing in more lead getters.

• Your product is so good that a third of your customers bring you more customers.

- Your executive team drives all this growth without you.

- And…*you have more engaged leads than you can possibly handle.*

This takes anywhere from five to ten years. Building something great, even if you know exactly what to do, takes time. It took my wife and I *more than ten years of our best effort,* to cross the first $100M in net worth. So the bigger your goals, the longer your time horizons need to be. You want to play games where if you wait, you win.

 **Alex Hormozi** ✔
@AlexHormozi

Entrepreneurship isn't for the faint of heart.

The load is heavy and the road is long.

FREE GIFT: BONUS TUTORIAL - Scaling from $0 to $100M+

Sometimes it's useful to hear a narrative of what each stage is like. If you know what comes next, you can start preparing for it today. I recorded a free tutorial where I help you identify where you are at, and what comes next so you can win. You can grab the tutorial free at, you guessed it, Acquisition.com/training/leads. As always, you can also scan the QR code below if you hate typing.

A Decade in a Page

"Simplicity is the ultimate sophistication" - Leonardo Da Vinci

We've covered a lot. And I think organizing what we learned into one place helps it sink in. So I made this "back of the napkin" list of what we've covered and why.

1) How to define a lead from this point forward. Now you know what you're after: engaged leads, not just leads.

2) How to turn leads into engaged leads with an offer or lead magnet. And, how to make them.

3) The *Core Four* - the only four ways we can let people know about the stuff we sell.

   a) How to reach out to people who know us: *ask them if they know anybody*

   b) How to post publicly: *hook, retain, reward. Give until they ask.*

   c) How to reach out to strangers: *lists, personalization, big fast value, volume*

   d) How to run paid ads to strangers: *targeting, callouts, What-Who-Whens, CTAs, client financed acquisition*

4) Maximizing the Core Four: *More Better New*

   a) What keeps us from doing what I'm currently doing at ten times the volume? Then solving for that.

   b) Finding the constraint in our advertising. Then testing until it frees the constraint. Then doing *more* until it gets constrained again.

5) The Four Lead Getters: *Customers, Employees, Agencies, and Affiliates*

   a) How to get customers to refer other customers

   b) How to get employees to scale your advertising without you

   c) How to get an agency to teach you new skills

   d) How to get affiliates launched and integrated

6) When advertising in the real world: *The Rule of 100 and Open to Goal*

   a) The five-step, one-page advertising plan is to get more leads *today*.

7) The seven levels of advertising and the *$100M leads* machine in action.

As I promised in the beginning, the result of these bullets is more, better, cheaper, reliable engaged leads. I hope this book provides you utility. I hope as a result of reading this you know how to get more leads than you currently are. And I hope I unmasked the mystery behind lead getting.

Also, since you are one of the few who actually finish what you start, I want to leave you with a parting gift: a fable that has gotten me through my hardest times.

The Many Sided Die

Imagine you and a friend play a dice-rolling game. You are each given one die. One of the die has 20 sides. The other has 200. On each die, only one side is green. And the rest, are red.

The point of the game is simple: *Roll green as many times as you can.*

The rules of the game are as follows:

- *You can't see how many sides you have. You can only see if you roll red or green.*

- *If you roll green—One of your red sides turns green, and you get to roll again.*

- *If you roll red—Nothing happens, and you get to roll again.*

- *The game ends when you stop rolling. And if you stop rolling, you lose.*

What do you do?

You roll. When you roll red, you pick up the die and roll again. When others roll green, you pick up your die and roll again. When you roll green, you pick up the die and roll again.

You keep telling yourself one thing. "The more I roll, the more greens I get." At first, you roll green once in a while. But as more red sides turn green, the greens happen more. With enough rolls, hitting green becomes the rule rather than the exception.

What does your friend do?

He rolls a few times and hits red each time. He sees you roll a green and complains that you *must* have a die with fewer sides. He reasons, it's the *only* way you could have rolled green before him. And although you did, you also rolled many more times. So which is it?

In either case, he rolls a few more times in frustration and hits a green. But then he complains about how long it took. He's spent more time watching you and complaining than actually playing. Meanwhile, you've hit your green streak. *It's so much easier for you*, he tells himself. *You get greens every time! This game is rigged, so what's the point?* He quits.

***

So who got the die with 20 sides? Who got the die with 200 sides? If you get the game then you see, once you roll enough times, *the die you're given doesn't matter.*

- Die with fewer sides might roll green sooner.

- Die with more sides might roll green later.

- But, a die with a green side *always* has a chance of rolling green… *if you roll it.*

- Every die hits its green streak when rolled enough times.

All of us get a many-sided die. And looking at the other players, you have no idea if it's their 100th roll or their 100,000th. You don't know how "good" other players are when they start, you can only see how well they do *now*. But, if you understand the game, you also know *it doesn't matter.*

A few begin playing early. Others begin much later. The rest sit on the sidelines complaining about how lucky the players are. I guess so, but they're luckier because they play. And when they hit red, which they do, they didn't quit. They rolled again.

Learning to advertise is a lot like the game of the many sided die. You do not know if it will work until you try. And when you start advertising, you will probably hit red on your first rolls. But if you try enough times *you will hit green.* And *when* it works, you have a better chance of getting it to work *again.* The more you do it, the easier it gets. You begin to understand the game.

No matter how many players there are or the number of sides on the die you're given, you start to see the only two guarantees:

1) The more times you roll, the better you get.

2) If you quit, you lose

So here's my final promise:

You cannot lose if you do not quit.

FREE GOODIES:
CALLS TO ACTION

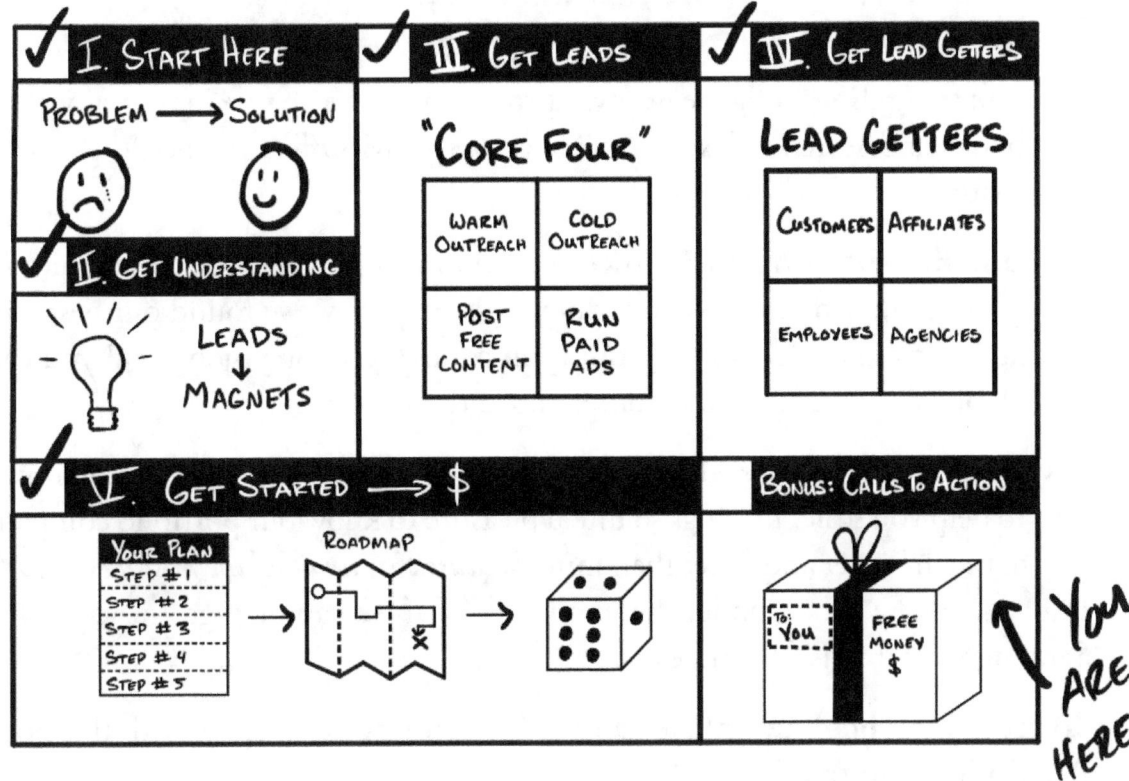

I'm gonna give you a bunch of free stuff in a second - so stay tuned.

Dr. Kashey (my editor) and I spent over 3,500 hours on this book. We wrote 650+ pages and 19 drafts with varying frames, themes, and points of focus. But ultimately, the changes left only the most distilled 'need to knows' inside. We went through 127 pages of hand drawn models to carve out the few that made it into the book. All that to say - I hope this work results in you growing the business of your dreams.

When I look back on my life these books will be among the things I am most proud of. I wouldn't be able to write as fervently if I didn't think people would read it. And as much as I strive to be the man who would work as hard if nobody cared, I am not there yet. Your support and positivity make a difference for me. So thank you from the bottom of my heart for allowing me to do the work I find meaningful. I am forever grateful.

If you are new to #mozination, welcome. We believe in big ambitions, and matching our ambitions with giving and patience. And I have a personal goal in that spirit of giving: *to die with nothing left to give.*

So if you're still with me, thank you. I want to provide some more goodies.

1) **If you're struggling to figure out <u>who</u> to sell to**, I released a chapter called "Your First Avatar" between this book and the last. Think of it like a 'single' from a music album. You can get it for free at <u>Acquisition.com/avatar.</u> Just pop in your email and we'll send it over.

2) **If you're struggling to figure out <u>what</u> to sell**, you can go to Amazon or wherever you buy books and search "Alex Hormozi" and $100M Offers. It should get you on the right path.

3) **If you want a job at Acquisition.com** or in one of our portfolio companies - we love hiring from #mozination. We love doing this because we've found our best returns investing in great people. Go to <u>Acquisition.com/careers/open-jobs</u>, and you can see all the job openings across all our companies and our portfolio.

4) **If your company is over $1M in EBITDA (profit)**, we'd love to invest in your business to help you scale. It brings so much pleasure to know our portfolio companies have grown much bigger and faster than mine *because they avoided the mistakes I made*. If you want us to take a look under the hood and see if we can help go to <u>Acquisition.com</u>. Sending your info is fast and easy.

5) To get the **free book downloads and video trainings** that come with this book, go to <u>Acquisition.com/training/leads</u>.

6) **If you like listening to podcasts and want to hear more**, my podcast at the time of this writing is top 5 in entrepreneurship and top 15 in business in the US. You can get there by searching "Alex Hormozi" wherever you listen. Or, by going to <u>Acquisition.com/podcast</u>. I share useful and interesting stories, valuable lessons, and the essential mental models I rely on every day.

7) **If you like to watch videos**, we put a lot of resources into our free training, available for everyone. We intend on making it better than any paid stuff out there, and let you decide if we succeeded. You can find our videos on YouTube or wherever you watch videos by searching "Alex Hormozi".

8) **And if you like short form videos**, check out the bite sized content we pump out on the daily at <u>Acquisition.com/media</u>. You'll see all the places we post and you can pick the ones you like the most.

And last, thank you again. Please be one of those givers and **share this with other entre-preneurs by leaving a review**. It would mean the world to me. I'm sending you business building vibes from my desk. I spend a lot of time there, so it's a lot of vibes. May your desire be greater than your obstacles.

Hope to meet you and your company soon. Ad astra.

Alex Hormozi, Founder, Acquisition.com

www.ingramcontent.com/pod-product-compliance
Lightning Source LLC
Chambersburg PA
CBHW080958120626

46546CB00010B/2943